To Te

D1168016

10 Ways to Screw Up an Ad Campaign

. . . and How to Create Ones That Work

Let's "rock" 'em!

Barry H. Cohen

A BUSINESS

Adams Media
Avon, Massachusetts

Previously published as *Ten Ways to Screw Up an Ad Campaign* by First Books Library, Indianapolis, IN, 2001

Published by
Adams Media, an F+W Publications Company
57 Littlefield Street, Avon, MA 02322. U.S.A.
www.adamsmedia.com

ISBN 10: 1-59869-082-5
ISBN 13: 978-1-59869-082-8
Printed in the United States of America

J I H G F E D C B A

Library of Congress Cataloging-in-Publication Data
Cohen, Barry H.
10 ways to screw up an ad campaign / by Barry H. Cohen.
p. cm.
Includes index.
ISBN 1-59869-082-5
1. Advertising. 2. Small business. I. Title. II. Title: Ten ways to screw up an ad campaign.

HF5823.C555 2006
659.1'13--dc22

2006014706

This publication is designed to provide accurate and authoritative information with regard to the subject matter covered. It is sold with the understanding that the publisher is not engaged in rendering legal, accounting, or other professional advice. If legal advice or other expert assistance is required, the services of a competent professional person should be sought.
—From a *Declaration of Principles* jointly adopted by a Committee of the American Bar Association and a Committee of Publishers and Associations

Many of the designations used by manufacturers and sellers to distinguish their product are claimed as trademarks. Where those designations appear in this book and Adams Media was aware of a trademark claim, the designations have been printed with initial capital letters.

Excerpts from *Please Be Ad-vised* and interview appearing in Chapter 16 reprinted with permission of Douglas J. Wood, Reed Smith, 599 Lexington Avenue, New York, NY, 10022.

This book is available at quantity discounts for bulk purchases.
For information, please call 1-800-872-5627.

Dedication

To my wife, Deborah, who acted as midwife during the delivery of this book.

Acknowledgments

First and foremost, I would like to thank Ken and Daria Dolan of the WOR Radio Network for their belief in me and in my work. Second, my thanks to Marla Markman and Lamont Wood for their guidance. A special thanks goes to Jeff Witchel for designing the cover of the first edition.

Many thanks to the fine folks at Adams Media for reissuing this book.

I would be remiss if I did not thank my many colleagues from the broadcast industry for embracing and recommending this book—especially the good folks at the Radio Advertising Bureau, the National Association of Broadcasters, and Interep.

I must thank Arnie Schwartz and Larry Conti for bringing me into this business we call advertising. You indeed provided the launching pad for this book.

A well-deserved (albeit posthumous) thanks goes out to J. Albert Wunder, who challenged me to break through all my self-imposed limits.

I can't say enough to that loyal group of clients that has followed me over the years. I will always be there for you as well.

To my business partner and friend of over twenty-five years, Bill Bird, thanks for assisting me at the seminars that became this book. Now we can share what we have learned with the rest of the entrepreneurs. Like these struggling go-getters, we have been there, bootstrapping it—a few missed meals and many missed paychecks.

To my parents, I thank you for imparting the survival skills that work in both business and in life. I only wish I had written this while my mother was still alive.

Last but not least, there is a God, without whom none of this is possible.

Thanks, Boss.
—Barry Cohen

Contents

Introduction

Most small businesses in America today are committing advertising suicide . . . the rest are playing a dangerous game of Russian roulette.

—Barry H. Cohen

It doesn't have to be that way. You're reading this, and I'm writing this, because we're committed to ending that situation. This guide is dedicated to the owners and operators of small businesses and professional practices everywhere. We're here together to explode the myths—to break through the barriers. In a few short hours, I pledge to give you the tools to compete more successfully . . . no matter what the industry, no matter how large, well-funded, or well-entrenched your adversaries.

This is a practical guide—intended for anyone, regardless of knowledge or skill level. I have taken the most frequent mistakes advertisers make, and presented them along with solutions that work. I challenge you to put them to work in your business or professional practice—immediately.

The first part of this book will address the most common mistakes made by small-business owners. The second part will provide you with a working manual to overcome those frequently made mistakes. You will find a glossary of terms in the back of the book, along with a recommended reading list. As you progress through the book, I will set apart useful tips we call "toolboxes." You will also find various sidebars to illustrate the points in the chapter. I will take you back to simpler times in my "Time Capsules." You will look at real-life marketing situations in an imaginary place called "The Highlight Zone."

Enough with the serious stuff—lighten up, and enjoy *10 Ways to Screw Up an Ad Campaign*.

part 1

THE 10 WAYS . . .

chapter 1

Hire Your Brother-in-Law as Marketing Director . . . Or Your Spouse

Would you hire your plumber to do your taxes?

Of course not. Then why would you consider entrusting the lifeblood of your business to anyone but a highly qualified professional?

Over the years, while selling advertising services to companies of all sizes, it has never ceased to amaze me how many unqualified people end up being responsible for this critical function. And don't deceive yourself—marketing is a critical function. Consider the following: Your accountant controls the money going out. Your marketing director controls the money coming in.

By choosing the right person for your marketing director, you can turn up the faucet on the incoming flow of money—the primary goal for your business.

So hiring the right marketing person is an investment, not an expense. The right person will know that marketing is not an excuse to impress his or her idea of culture or wit upon the masses. He or she will not simply bludgeon them with your logo in the name of brand awareness. That person will not make mistakes so dumb that they will be remembered long after the product itself has achieved some dignity through death. It's not only small business that has committed the blunders; some of the best and the brightest companies have contributed some of the biggest boondoggles in marketing history. Consider:

- When Coca-Cola launched its product in China, learned the hard way that the popular U.S. slogan "Coke Adds Life" translated to "Coke brings your dead ancestors to life," in Chinese. It got attention—but it did not sell beverages.
- When Clairol attempted to introduce its curling iron, the "Mist Stick," into Germany, they discovered that "mist" is slang for manure in German. Not too many people wanted to buy a manure stick.
- When Coors, the great brewer from Golden, Colorado, attempted to translate its slogan "Turn It Loose" into Spanish, it translated to "Suffer from Diarrhea."
- In American usage, "nova" means a new, bright star—quite a catchy name for a car. When the Chevy Nova was put on sale in Latin America, someone realized that *no va* is Spanish for "to not go"—the absolute worst name for a car. Unless, of course, you're one of the few who bought an Edsel, one of the auto industry's greatest design failures.

The right marketing person will not blunder like this because the right person will understand that marketing is more than coining slogans that make the boss happy. That person will understand the real meaning of marketing.

WHAT IS MARKETING?

Marketing means aligning the way you sell and/or move goods and services through a distribution system to the end user with the way your customers buy. Knowing this, proper marketing amounts to a form of sales insurance. Rather than doing some things, and then, if they work, doing them again, effective marketing means doing the right thing, with the right product, at the right time. And, in the process, avoiding costly mistakes.

The marketing professional does this by asking the right questions. You got it—the whole process is controlled by market research, which boils down to an attempt to ask intelligent questions (and then get them answered). Questions like:

- Who buys this product?
- What makes this product different and better than its competition?
- Where do the buyers shop?
- What do the buyers like, how much do they spend, what do they do in their spare time, etc.?

When the Spalding Company launched the Top Flite XL II golf ball, it sent out a group of professional marketers—myself included—to interview golfers. Countless hours were spent talking to prospective customers. By the end of the process, Spalding knew what balls their prospects used and why, how many balls they used, how often they played, where they bought their balls, and how much they were willing to pay—and every other piece of information that seemed pertinent.

Of course, the new product succeeded.

You probably can't afford to undertake anything as elaborate as Spalding's research efforts—but don't let that bother you. You may not be able to send out squads of marketing ninjas, but you can scope out the lay of the land before taking a swing at attracting customers to your business. Having said that, remember that a little knowledge is a dangerous thing, since it can delude you into thinking that you actually know more than you do. Secure in the knowledge that your product sold okay in the United States, you can wake up one morning to find yourself loading thousands of Chevy Novas on ships bound for South America.

But one little fact-finding mission, carried out by someone who knows the pitfalls and blind alleys, can tell you how to price a product and where to advertise it. The right person can determine in advance, using focus groups, whether the product name you had your heart set on will generate sales, or gales of derision.

Think of an advertising campaign as a lightning rod, bringing energy into your business. If that rod is solidly grounded in marketing, it will charge up your enterprise. If not, it will burn it to a crisp.

DON'T PASS THE HAT

Even if your company is small and someone with other responsibilities will wear the marketing hat, make sure that hat fits. Ask yourself:

- Has this person had any contact with your customers, or with people that buy a similar product?
- Does he or she have experience working with outside advertising suppliers?
- Does this person have any established relationships with suppliers of marketing services?
- Most importantly, does this person have any marketing success stories?

If you don't ask these questions, you may end up like a client I had years ago, a family-owned three-store retail operation. Every two years, they passed the advertising baton to someone else. Yes, the new person always brimmed with fresh ideas and approaches, and gained experience that rounded out his or her value to the operation. But in the final analysis, none of them were advertising professionals. And thanks to the family's two-year rotation policy, they were completing their learning curve at exactly the time they were called on to pass the baton to another novice. They all received an education, but the operation probably paid more for those educations (indirectly, through bungled marketing) than if the recipients had been sent to the Harvard Business School.

Another tendency in small companies is to throw the marketing hat at the sales manager. After all, he or she is involved with both the customers and the products. Except there's one problem: The CEO usually insists that the sales manager concentrates on making sales, since otherwise the organization may not be able to make its payroll the next Friday. So marketing, which may not produce results for months, is forgotten.

But there are even worse ways of doing marketing—you can do it with a committee. According to Jeff Witchel, owner of Witchel Advertising in East Brunswick, New Jersey, "Design by committee is the kiss of death for an ad." Too many cooks spoil the broth—especially when none of them wear chef's hats. He should know. Witchel has worked on campaigns for major food products, including Jell-O pudding and Grape Nuts Cereal, as well as prestigious travel and tourism clients such as Eastern Airlines, Pan Am, and Princess Tours.

THE ART OF HIRING

So, you're convinced. You'll hire a marketing professional. What do you look for first?

First, don't look, *listen*. You can find the marketing guru of your dreams by listening to the right mantra. Ask yourself:

- Does your candidate talk about airy-fairy forecasts, projections, and reports? Or does the candidate talk about better ways to sell your company's products?
- Does he or she sound like a graduate school textbook? Or do you hear talk of real-world, roll-up-the-sleeves, get-down-to-business action?

- Does the candidate talk about grand, historic, global trends? Or does he or she have a finger on the pulse of your industry, and of the business climate right now?
- Does the candidate seem concerned with bureaucratic schemes to create a department and spend money? Or is the candidate focused on ways to sell more of your product, and on ways to use your business's resources better?

Your ideal marketing person may be right under your nose. It could be someone who sells for one of your suppliers. Or it could be that talented person across town who's "eating your lunch" working for a competitor.

Always remember, youth loves a challenge—and there may be some young hotshots working for a competitor who don't see any way to move up where they are. You can give them a new career path. Look for somebody lean and hungry, someone who has not reached his or her comfort zone.

Next time you open your industry's trade magazine or newsletter, see who's kicking up dust. Notice the people getting awards at conferences and trade shows. Let them know you've noticed their work.

Don't be afraid to recruit in unconventional ways. As a general manager of a radio station in northern Virginia, I needed outside advertising salespeople. Classified ads did not bring quality results, so I called managers at larger noncompeting stations in nearby Washington, D.C. "Surely, you have applicants you don't have room for, or who aren't ready for you yet. Send them to me," I suggested. Within the hour, my fax machine began ringing with resumes of qualified candidates.

Assuming you've heard from qualified applicants whose mantra turned out to be what you wanted to hear, what now? Which one will you hire?

First, examine your own prejudices. The law aside, have you discounted an applicant in your own mind because of age, sex, race, or nationality? Don't let any of these groundless excuses hold you back.

A person you have nothing in common with could be just the right person to take your company forward.

Beyond that, you can actually test candidates. Gerald Getz, manager for the Sinclair Radio Group in the Scranton, Pennsylvania, region, asked each of his final contenders how they would increase sales at one property—the underperformer in his group. Each candidate received an overnight courier package with the complete scenario, including all the data needed to make recommendations.

UNIVERSAL PRINCIPLES

As we move along, you'll find that it doesn't matter what business you're in, or how long you've operated, or how large or small your business is; the same principles apply:

- Decide what you sell.
- Figure out who buys it.
- Figure out how to find them.
- Talk to them.
- Determine why they should buy from you.
- Examine your delivery system.
- Essentially, tell them your story.
- Say it loud; say it proud.
- Invite them in.
- Please them.
- Invite them back.

TOOLBOX

Select a marketing person who understands your business so well that he or she could step up and take over should you need to step down.

Find the right person to beat the drum for you. Then, give them a drum and stand back. Sound too simple? It's not. I'll show you how, step by step.

THOUGHTS ABOUT HIRING RELATIVES

Remember one thing about your family: You can't fire them. Well, you may, after enormous agony, manage to confront them about their non-performance and convince them to step aside. But even then, they don't go away. You're still related to them. You still have to live with them, or at the very least, see them at family gatherings. But resentment may color every interaction you have with them from then on—you may see it in every glance and remark.

You may think you have the exception to the "don't hire family" rule. Your brother-in-law took a couple of marketing courses in college, twenty years ago. Putting him in charge might actually work out. You could fire him if you had to, you think, while taking comfort in the thought that you probably won't have to. But remember this phrase: "Familiarity breeds contempt." I use this phrase *not* in reference to the familiarity between two relatives, but familiarity with the business. He may be too emotionally close to the company, to the status quo, or to you, to really see what's going on and to take action when a situation demands change. In other words, even if you can fire the proverbial brother-in-law, he may not feel that he can talk back to you or ask serious questions about the system you set up before he arrived. Fresh pairs of eyes and ears can bring a lot to the table. It's worth the effort to recruit them.

In the introduction, I said most small businesses were committing advertising suicide; while the rest were playing Russian roulette. The disaster starts with people—when you have the wrong ones. Raise the importance of the marketing function in your organization. Treat it like gold.

◀◀ Time Capsule: "Eat at Grunt's"

Let's take the first of those trips that were promised in the introduction, trips back in time to (seemingly) simpler eras. Let's start with the first advertising campaign—caveman-style.

Let's have the time machine take us to Grunt's, a restaurant with a very cave-like ambiance. Well, it *is* a cave. It's truly unique—it's the only restaurant in the valley. The food is notably fresh—today, they're serving freshly killed brontosaurus from the valley's bronto stockyards.

But Mr. Grunt, proprietor, is *not* content to wait for the natural charms and qualities of his establishment to win over a clientele. Ignoring complaints from his mate that the fire is not ready yet, he ascends the hillside and takes a deep breath.

"Aaaaayyyaaaaya-ah-ah! Aaaaayyyaaaaya-ah-ah!"

It echoes off the canyon walls, and the tribesmen gather. They know a "weekly special" notice when they hear it.

Crude? Not really. Consider:

Grunt has defined his trading area: the canyon settlement, his cave, and the stockyards. He appears to have a lock on both the supply and the demand, with a captive crowd. He enjoys an inexpensive delivery system and a great broadcast outlet. And his message communicates a passionate belief in the quality of his product. Admittedly, it communicates little else—but what more do you need?

Well, maybe someone less emotionally involved in the business to handle the marketing—that fire *really* wasn't ready.

Candidly, there are other considerations a marketer might also want to ponder—but we'll get into those as we get deeper into the book. ▶▶

chapter 2

Hire the Biggest Ad Agency in Town . . . When You're the Smallest Advertiser in Town

Thinking of hiring an ad agency? Wonderful. Now, put down the phone. Close the Yellow Pages. There is something you must understand before launching your search: One of the worst things you can do is run out and hire the biggest agency in town, simply because of their size.

Size offers no automatic advantage—the billboards are not any bigger, the TV commercials are not any louder. No one will be impressed by the fact that you are using Mega Agency, since hardly anyone will ever know (or care). In fact, as I'll discuss, size can offer some disadvantages.

In reality, however, there are so many factors to consider when choosing an agency that you might indeed end up hiring the largest one in town—if it offers the best fit for you. Then again, the smallest could turn out to be the best choice.

But first, there's the bigger question: Do you need an advertising agency at all?

The answer is that, usually, you do—especially if you are spending significant amounts of money compared to other advertisers in your market. (However, advertising costs vary so much from large cities to small towns that it won't work to say that you should get an agency if you spend more than X dollars.)

By hiring an agency, you stand to benefit from someone else's experience. Without experience, you will end up relying on the advice of the advertising salespeople of the media you plan to advertise with—hardly an unbiased opinion. An ad agency should be able to offer greater breadth of experience than many media salespeople.

Left to yourself, you might be able to tell the story of your business, to compose a gripping *who-what-where-when-and-how* narrative to put in front of potential customers. But how do you find those potential customers? What part of the story do you put in front of them? Where do you tell it? When will you tell them? What response can you expect?

The "where" is especially troublesome for beginners confronting the "media maze" out there: national TV, local TV, radio, direct mail, trade magazines, consumer magazines, industrial magazines, daily newspapers, weekly newspapers, billboards, Web sites, sky writing, blimps, Little League uniforms, bus stop benches, mall hand-selling, door knob flyers, infomercials.

Ready to scream? Then an ad agency may be the answer. With an agency, you can acquire a team of experts who can quickly get you through this maze and let you get back to business.

But first, you have to choose the agency that's right *for you*. Let's look at some of the things you need to consider.

SIZE DOES MATTER

One size does not fit all. Put a six-year-old on a ten-speed racing bike, and what happens? It could be the best bike made, full of all the gadgets that bicyclists yearn for—but the child will crash, and the crash could have been prevented.

Similarly, when an advertiser and an agency meet, they must have a good fit. Your first consideration should be the size of the agency. Small clients get lost in large ad agencies. They either receive little attention or are shunted off to "Johnny Junior" account executive.

In the early 1990s, I worked at an ad agency that received a call from a client dissatisfied with his present agency. His budget was significant—more than $400,000 a year. Still, he felt he did not receive the attention he required. You see, many of the other clients at that agency spent millions annually on their advertising.

TOOLBOX

Look for an ad agency willing to invest in *your* business's long-term growth. Avoid a firm looking to line its pockets. No matter how much you like their work, if you can't afford their work, keep looking.

AFTER SIZE, QUALIFICATIONS

After you decide what size agency best suits your needs, consider the following factors.

Dinosaurs Need Not Apply . . .

Unfortunately, advertising practitioners come in all shapes, sizes, capabilities, and (sadly) ethics. Nearly anyone can hang out a shingle. There is no licensing process in the ad agency business. Agencies don't have to pass a competency exam. (If they did, we could quickly thin out their ranks.) Today, it is not uncommon for legitimate ad agencies to even carry errors and omissions insurance.

So how do you penetrate the façade and find out what they really know? Try these moves:

Ask to see resumes or bios of the principals. Their backgrounds indicate the agency's main areas of interest and competence.

Ask who will service your account. What level and depth of experience do they have? What books have they read on the subject? If they can't name at least a few titles on my recommended reading list in Appendix A, keep looking.

Ask for references. What satisfied clients do they have in your community? Do their clients have a similar profile to your business? Do they have experience in your industry, or will your business provide their "learning curve"? Peter Caroline, of Write on Target in Green Valley, Arizona, advises, "You have to talk the talk and walk the walk. In any field, you must know the product, and have a feel for it." Caroline should know; he has a depth of expertise in firearms. His self-promotional piece intones, "If your advertising is aimed at shooters, shouldn't a shooter be writing it?"

What policies do they have concerning the handling of competing clients? Can you negotiate an exclusive contract for your product category within your trading area? I used to marvel at how many financial and retail automotive advertisers would use the same ad agency—with two artists side-by-side, creating ads for direct competitors. You deserve a certain amount of confidentiality regarding your business's strategy.

How much of their work does the agency actually perform themselves, and how much do they outsource to freelancers, production companies, and other suppliers? You may find yourselves paying large markups for a "virtual" company that simply acts as a coordinator.

Ask about results, not awards. Agencies love to enter contests. Alas, an ad campaign that wins awards does not necessarily sell products. Remember, you want to increase your return on your advertising investment—over what you would have brought in had you handled the advertising yourself.

Ask to see their "book" (their portfolio of print ads) and their commercial demo reel. They don't have one? Be suspicious of graphics houses masquerading as ad agencies. In today's world, an agency with no electronic media background is too one-dimensional to help you stay ahead of your competition.

What is the ratio of money spent on ads vs. money spent creating the ads? If your budget is small, beware the agency that spends so much creating the ads that you can't afford to do much with them. If that is the case, look elsewhere, because this agency is looking for fees and markups. They're more interested in their bottom line than yours. (As a general rule of thumb, expect to spend roughly 15 percent of your budget to create the material and 85 percent on ad space or airtime.) I have devoted as much as *95 percent* of a client's budget to buying radio time—and still produced quality commercials with only 5 percent of the ad budget.

My company recently presented against an agency that brought in a ringer—a hired gun with big agency credentials. They promised the client that this individual, who claimed credit for authorship of some high-profile national campaigns, would work on their account. They then proceeded to strong-arm the client into giving them the whole account, including a direct-response broadcast advertising project, "to avoid charging them large creative fees." The result: They ran an improperly executed campaign that produced dismal results. They simply did not have the necessary expertise in direct-response broadcast advertising. The client learned the hard way; they ran out of money, later admitting that we could have done a better job. The moral of the story: Don't get taken in by the flash.

TOOLBOX

When looking for an ad agency, don't just look in the Yellow Pages. First go to someone at a media outlet that you use, and ask who does good work.

NEXT: CREDITWORTHINESS

This is indeed an important consideration. You have to understand that your ad agency will be handling your money. Therefore, you need to be confident that they will handle it with the same care, attention, and integrity that you would. Since most ad agencies act in a fiduciary capacity, their practices can affect how the media perceives your business. If the agency "floats" your money and pays the media late—or fails to pay them—it could cost you serious dollars. Worse yet, it could cost you your reputation. Check the media that the agency does business with for references.

Years ago, one small agency used to collect from its accounts, then invest its clients' media dollars in six-month certificates of deposit before paying their media bills. This "float" practice is commonly called "kiting." The media never shared in this little extra profit scheme. I doubt that the clients did either.

➡Martha Capps: "How Does My Network Grow?"

Go West, young man . . . or Midwest, young lady. Martha Capps, principal of the Capps Companies in Eden Prairie, Minnesota, did just that. A one-person marketing consultant, Capps outsources much of her work to a well-developed and highly trusted network of practitioners. She herself concentrates on the strategic planning aspects of her clients' campaigns.

Capps cites these advantages to working this way:

1. Clients always work with the principal.
2. She always becomes involved hands-on with the implementation of every campaign.
3. She brings the perspective of having worked in various regions.

Capps cites these advantages over working with a traditional agency, but is quick to caution the advertiser to "be sure the person really has the experience and the contacts." She also points to the need for a sole practitioner to "become an extension of the client's staff," which she mentions comes from developing a long-term relationship— an important element in her effectiveness.

You're Hiring, Not Buying

When you conduct an agency review, handle it as you would an employee search. Interview the best candidates. Let your staff have some input into the selection process; they may have to work with the agency. Pit one competitor against another. Often, they will do "spec" (speculative) campaigns, in order to win your business.

These days, large corporations often dole out separate assignments to different agencies, according to their strengths. A company may award the consumer portion of their account to one agency, while hiring another to handle their business-to-business advertising. You can, too.

I worked with a high-end retail jeweler for about seven years. Much to one of their agencies' chagrin, the client awarded me the broadcast portion of their account. The other shop handled their print ads. This arrangement served the advertiser's best interest.

THE AFTERGLOW

Okay, you followed my advice, and hired an agency you feel comfortable with. Now, the work begins. Here are a few suggestions to keep a well-oiled relationship with your ad counsel.

TOOLBOX

When looking for an ad agency, your own industry trade association may be able to make a referral. Do not rely on the names you find in advertising trade magazines; often, only larger agencies will be mentioned there.

Test-drive them. Give an agency a small project before committing your entire account to them. If they handle the assignment well, give them a short-term commitment. Once you are satisfied, turn the balance of the business over to them. *Grow into the relationship.*

Ask, "What have you done for me lately?" Together with the agency decide, up front, how and when you will measure the agency's performance. A periodic review is a good idea for both of you—but keep in mind that changing agencies like socks will do little to advance your position in the marketplace. Give them a reasonable amount of time—at least six months—to adjust to how your business operates. Expect them to act as an extension of your staff. At one agency I worked for, we sat in on the client's sales meetings, and even observed transactions on the sales floor. Another agency I know sends out an annual report card to its clients, asking, "How are we doing?"

Address problems early. Don't wait until they get out of hand. Start by asking for an organizational chart. Do they have a backup representative to your primary contact? Then find out who the other team members are and how to contact each when you need them. Expect reasonable turnaround times, but be reasonable with your deadlines.

Clarify financial terms up front. Every agency I have worked for or operated presents its clients with a detailed cost estimate of every job. Work begins only after the client signs off on the estimate. That way, there are no surprises when the bill comes.

THE ENDGAME

If things don't work out, you can tell your ad agency goodbye. And they can do the same. Any number of reasons can cause either party to want to bail out—the client outgrows the agency; the agency doesn't deliver as promised; or the client doesn't pay its bills in a timely fashion.

Just make the split in a reasonable and respectful manner. Both the client and the ad agency can help or hurt each other. A "no-fault divorce" is the way to go. Make this part of your understanding.

Try to have a wind-down period, during which you pay for all outstanding invoices and get back any master tapes, layouts, etc. Generally, unless your agreement says otherwise, the client owns the creative product—once he or she pays the agency for it. I have seen many client-agency disputes arise because the parties initially failed to specify ownership clearly. An ad agency relationship is like a marriage—these days, a prenuptial agreement makes sense. And if you find your business on the "dating circuit" again, you'll be much wiser about what to look for in your next advertising partner.

➡ A Message from the Grim Reaper

Be warned that in advertising, as in most creative fields, the value of a business deal is often founded on the personal relationship between the participants. It is tempting to leave it that way and not formalize the relationship. And, indeed, informality will work—until something goes wrong, such as a partner dying, or leaving unexpectedly.

You will discover that, if you had formalized the relationship and committed your intentions to paper, something might be salvaged. Otherwise, things come to a standstill until a new relationship is established.

ATTENTION, CLASS

So what have we learned? You've decided to get help—good decision. You've looked around; you've asked around, you've done the "cattle call." Now that the dog and pony shows are over, it's time to make a choice. Make it wisely, but remember—it doesn't have to be forever. You're not looking for Picasso or Shakespeare; you need ad counsel that understands how to sell your product. Make them prove themselves. Expect a more effective strategy than you came up with yourself. If you don't see results in a reasonable period of time, respectfully part company.

➡ "So You Want to Run an Ad Campaign?"

Here's the situation: Company A wants to launch its new retail cosmetic, health, and beauty aid store chain. The stores appeal to eighteen-to thirty-four-year-old working women. Congratulations—you're in charge of advertising the launch.

You try ads in the local daily newspapers. And the results are dismal—you discover that the target audience doesn't read newspapers.

Okay, there's always television. But you find that they're out shopping or socializing during prime time.

So you try putting ads on the dance/rock radio stations, aimed at commuters. And the results are still dismal—someone points out that in your metropolitan area the suburban women you are trying to reach commute mainly by train, where the radio can't reach them.

"Billboards," you think—they can still see billboards. Except the environmentalists had them all torn down recently.

So there you are at a management meeting, laying out your last, desperate idea: placards inside the commuter trains. The transit authority will be happy to lease you the display space, right beside the public health warnings.

Or, you can hold that meeting to decide what ad agency you want to hire, and outsource the whole problem to a team of experts. The choice (and the ulcers, the migraines, and the career damage) is yours.

chapter 3

Do What You've Always Done . . . And You'll Get What You've Always Gotten— And No More

Times change. People change. Fashions change. And your advertising has to influence the same fickle public, which has itself experienced countless changes while discarding countless fads.

You can do it—you just have to embrace change.

For instance, maybe your father had an appliance store on Main Street. A handsome sign marked it, and he advertised in the evening newspaper. But:

- The sign was enough to draw in anyone on their way to the town square. And everyone went there. Now, appliances are sold in discount stores on the highway, and the highway bypasses the downtown—and the store—entirely.
- The older customers who were the mainstay of the business have gotten even older. In fact, they have died off or moved to retirement homes, and certainly are not buying new appliances.
- The last guy to come home and read the evening newspaper was probably Ward Cleaver. Evening papers are dinosaurs, and even morning papers have seen Monday through Saturday circulation decline. Only Sundays are holding on.

So, do you just fold the tent and creep away, dismayed at being trapped in this world you didn't make? *Of course not.* You change your advertising and media strategies. You seek to generate traffic to make up for your isolation. You address a new generation of homeowners. You supplement your newspaper ads with other media.

But more than anything else, you keep in mind the situation of today's consumers: They are faced with enormous poverty.

MODERN POVERTY

I'm not talking about breadlines and hobo jungles. In today's world, your customers face "time poverty." Mr. and Mrs. America both work outside the home. After work, they're both ferrying kids between Little League practice, violin lessons, and karate school. She goes to night school and aerobics classes. He goes to racquetball and bowling.

They're moving targets—so how do you hit them? More specifically, how do you reach these people with your message when their own affairs demand nearly all their attention?

You get creative. You break with tradition. You find new solutions. You face the fact that if your market research is correct and your best prospects have green hair, visible tattoos, and pierced chins, you need to sponsor a rock concert. (If you discreetly wear your earplugs, no one will know.)

And now we come to the place where I have to tell you that there are answers that you can't look up in the back of the book. Having told you the importance of doing things differently, and of the need to reach people who can barely steal a glance at billboards, I have to break it to you that there is no pat solution. If there were, advertisers would do it over and over until a sickened public recoiled—as with certain car or long-distance ads—again forcing you to try something new.

I can, however, offer you these successful examples, hoping they will trigger some inspiration.

JEFF'S UNBREAKABLE WATERBEDS

Around the dawn of time (1970), one of my clients opened one of the first stores on the East Coast to sell waterbeds. For years, he got away with the unimaginative practice of advertising $99 waterbeds in the Sunday paper—perfect for impulse buyers. When customers walked in, he'd sell them a better, costlier item. That's what they call "bait and switch," and it may or may not be legal, depending on where you live.

In time, it stopped working—the waterbed-buying public became more sophisticated and would not take the bait. Waterbeds became a serious purchase for younger buyers, who did research before purchasing. And they were likely to end up in one of the many waterbed franchise stores that began cropping up. They weren't necessarily more ethical, but they surrounded Jeff's store like a wagon train.

So, Jeff called me, and together, we created the first ever "Break the Bed Contest."

I had learned from his in-store posters that the biggest objection to buying a waterbed from first-time buyers was the "breakage myth." They were afraid the bed would leak and flood their homes.

So we created a dramatic hands-on (actually, feet-on) demonstration designed to explode the myth—but not the bed. We set up a bed in the parking lot and invited a disc jockey and a traffic reporter from the local rock radio station to jump on the bed during rush hour. During a live broadcast from the store, they invited the audience to a challenge—come on down, break the bed, and win a $500 gift certificate to the store.

We sold some beds. You can, too.

TOOLBOX

Try this: Name five ways that your customers or your marketplace have changed. Then devise at least two advertising strategies to address each change.

PROFITABLE FREE LUNCHES

Another of my clients was a very successful restaurant chain. It seemed as though everything they touched turned to gold—with little or no advertising. At least, it seemed that way for a while.

While they had a unique concept, in time the national chains began to move in on their territory with similar restaurants. That's when they asked for my help.

The restaurant chain's home state was New Jersey. That's also the home state of Bruce Springsteen, then in the midst of his "Born in the U.S.A." tour. So I arranged for the chain to sponsor live reports from a concert. The coverage included commercial announcements offering a free entree to anyone presenting a concert ticket stub at one of the restaurants.

The result: in one week, 856 documented responses. True, these free entrees cost the chain more than the advertising. However, the client had enough foresight to see the value of introducing new customers to their establishments. Besides, most patrons brought at least one other person, and ordered appetizers, drinks, and desserts along with those free entrees. And then they came back, repeatedly, as paying customers.

Remember, it's never a question of how much advertising you buy. It's a question of what you do to make it perform for your business. What is the selling strategy behind the ad campaign? *What will it do to drive traffic to your business?*

TOOLBOX

Front and center! Build both a "call to action" and a strong "incentive to action" into every ad, and you'll get action.

COUSIN MEETS WORLD

My cousin was an average student at best. In high school, no one thought of him as the most likely to succeed. Twenty years later, he built himself and his family a 4,200-square-foot house. Rich's unique success centers around his ability to sense changes in the marketplace and his industry, make decisions, and respond to them.

He started out selling CB radios—and you're probably bracing yourself for a woeful tale of bankruptcy, since the retail CB radio market is now considered a classic case of boom, saturation, and bust. But he saw himself as being in the mobile electronics market, so when saturation set in he was able to sidestep into police, fire, and marine radio. Later, he got into mobile phones—long before cellular came along.

Change is certain. Ask any CB radio salesman.

NAME THAT BUSINESS

Remembering what business you're in can give you some protection against change. After all, if the passenger railroads had realized that they were in the transportation business, they'd still be around today—because they would be operating the airlines.

Similarly, if you are in the pool business, are you in the business of digging holes and lining them with cement, or are you in the business of giving families a specific recreational experience? With this in mind, I once told one of my retail clients in the pool and spa business that his real competition was not the other pool stores. Rather, it was the travel agents. Both were courting the same discretionary funds from families that yearned to experience water sports.

So we fashioned his ad copy around the theme of "the vacation that lasts a lifetime." We argued that if you buy a pool, you have it next year, and for years to come. If you go on a cruise, all you have next year is snapshots.

You may not be selling pools, but the same line of argument applies to plenty of other products, such as motorcycles, where the advertiser is competing for the consumer's disposable income. The trick is to look beyond the merchandise and see what personal experience the customer is trying to buy. Then, make sure you're supplying it.

CONVENIENCE IS (ALMOST) EVERYTHING

With the shopping public being strapped for time and attention, it's no mystery that a high percentage of supermarket purchases are actually nonfood items. The customers have to buy groceries anyway, so why should they take the additional time to go to a drugstore, a hardware store, and a housewares store if the grocery store is smart enough to offer the same goods?

Convenience rules. So, surely, it would be hopeless for a shoe store in Bucks County, Pennsylvania, to attract patrons from across the Delaware River in Trenton, New Jersey. They would have to drive farther *and* pay a bridge toll. Except that a shoe store owner I knew advertised that he would pay the bridge tolls of any customers who would (like George Washington) make the crossing and present their toll receipts. They did.

Convenience rules—but there are always other factors you can bring into play, and attract your fair share (better yet, your unfair share) of business.

BE DIFFERENT

Dennis Adams, an auto dealer with several Dodge and Chrysler franchises in a number of counties throughout northern and central New Jersey, bought into a sleepy little country car dealership. His partner was known to prop his cowboy boots up on the desk, waiting for someone to drop in. But Dennis was not one for waiting.

So he renamed the place the "Cooga Mooga Auto Shopping Center," a name that cut through the clutter of "ad noise-eum" and got noticed. And the world began beating a path to the dealership—after he also did some high-profile advertising.

Suddenly, his partner was no longer napping at his desk. And all Dennis did was dare to be different—different enough to get people's attention.

¿SE HABLA HUH?

Since you are reading this, it's safe to assume that you read English. But let me break this to you gently: not everyone does.

I once worked in an ad agency that was dedicated to bringing in new accounts. In the process, they pitched the same high-profile automotive advertisers that all the other ad agencies pursued. One day, the boss's son dropped a thick proposal on my desk. It was from a corporation that had just bought a major group of car dealerships. Our agency was well qualified in the retail automotive field and had a good chance of winning the business. Unfortunately, the same thing could be said for many of our competitors.

"It's missing one major thing," I remarked. "There's no Spanish media." Yet, they were operating in one of the largest Spanish-speaking communities in the Northeast.

I added provisions for Spanish media to the proposal. And we won the account.

A MODEST PROPOSAL

The only things these stories have in common is that they involved change—someone profiting by doing something differently. And the very act of doing something differently forced them to be creative.

Change is inevitable, but it can be seen as an opportunity rather than a problem—an opportunity to be creative.

But what changes should you make, when, where, and how? Those are answers you can't look up in the back of the book. They are unique to you.

Since this is the end of the chapter, I'll succumb to temptation and present one specific change that you might want to make—because every business in America ought to make it.

It involves letting you in on a little secret: *Americans want to come back to Main Street, but Main Street has to welcome them back.*

Consider: People are tired of the lack of service they get from chain stores, malls, and large companies. They want to go back to Main Street—that place where they used to get personal, small-town service. But pure nostalgia won't bring them back—Main Street has to welcome them back.

Figure out what you are going to do differently to welcome them back, and you'll have fulfilled the premise of this chapter. You'll have changed.

TOOLBOX

Even if your product looks exactly like everyone else's, your level of service can still surpass theirs. Make sure it does, and then advertise the fact, and you will succeed.

❰❰ Time Capsule: "Eat at Attila's"

Time to revisit our eternal restaurant, whose marketing is based on principles that remain applicable despite the passage of time. In Chapter 1 we visited Grunt's, and saw how simplicity can mask sophistication. Today, our time machine takes us to a place with subtly different ambiance, one that earns the name "Wild Boar."

No, that's not their marketing logo—that is what's cooking. And the patrons in metal helmets and leather tunics—they too have a certain boorish air about them, but the problem is that they can't decide if they really want to eat there. They had wild boar yesterday. Then a waitress with the big ratty hair, carrying the big pot, passes among them, offering a taste. They decide to go in. A well-armed maitre d' takes their skins as they go in—no collection problems here.

Competition arises—that guy who yelled "duck!" was not ordering fowl, but reacting to an incoming spear. But that gives us the opportunity to observe how proprietor Attila responds . . . with swords! Refreshingly direct, don't you think?

But notice the neat layout of Attila's place; a greeter leads you in to the tent, where you get your own pot. This guy's a smart merchandiser. When things are slow, he relies on his private club to pull them in. (Which would be rough on the patrons were they not wearing helmets.)

Meanwhile, at the top of the hill, guys are waving torches. (The rental place would not have searchlights for another 3,000 years.) See the women, as they all exit the tent, telling others about Attila's. Here's the real corker; couples leaving with the boar bones in doggie bags.

It may look a little rough around the edges, but Attila's represents advanced, multimedia advertising. Combine the power of sampling, signage, searchlights, and word-of-mouth, and you've got a winning campaign.

Attila knows that your advertising is only as good as your service. If you deliver the goods at or above their expectations, your customers will advertise for you—no swords needed. **»**

chapter 4

Handle Everything Yourself . . . and You'll Be Out of Business

Somebody once said, "God gave us two ears, but only one mouth, for a reason." We may presume that the reason is that we should listen twice as much as we talk. Remember this sound advice.

You'll need this gem now that you've decided what business you're in, found a location, chosen a name, and prepared to tell the world about it. What should you do next?

Your next step should be finding help with your advertising.

The key here is for you to run *your* business. If you're spending your time playing Shakespeare, composing your ads or meeting with a Light Brigade of ad salespeople instead of taking care of your customers, you won't have any customers.

You can call it "outsourcing" or just "trusting a professional," but the idea is to have a team working for you—without having to pay for a benefits package or payroll taxes. You can accomplish that by using a full-service ad agency, or by hiring talented freelancers.

To find these people, contact your local ad club and check online. You may even find a directory of available talent local to your area. They're anxious to be hired, and employing them will allow you to focus on your business.

Even if you're just starting your business and don't have much money to work with, you still have the creative resources of the media. Most newspapers, magazines, radio stations, billboard companies, direct-mail houses, and cable companies offer some level of in-house creative staff. Often, the service comes with your purchase of ad space or time buy—at little or no cost to you. Now, the challenge may be to find the time to work with the ad people you have hired.

Unless you are a sole practitioner, *delegate*. Let a talented subordinate work with the media representatives, agency, or freelancers to develop your campaign. Just remember to empower them—and then leave the final decision to you. Set aside one hour every Wednesday night to review the next week's campaign. Allow for extra time in case changes need to be made. Respect the media's deadlines, and they'll respect yours.

TOOLBOX

Looking for ad talent? Find out who just got fired. It's a business where people often lose their jobs for reasons that have nothing to do with job performance.

HANDS OFF, OR HANDS ON?

You get the ad layout from your advertising people. You see picky little changes you'd like to make. Think—do you really have to make them?

Take my advice: **When you meet with your ad people, check your ego at the door.** While it's your nickel and your business, they're the experts.

I've seen clients destroy good work in what became an expensive game of Simon Says. "Simon says, 'Do this. Do that. Make it bigger. Move it to the left. Make the music louder.'"

Once you decide to hire advertising counsel, let them do the job. Imagine throwing the contractor out of the cement mixer before he builds your swimming pool. That's what advertisers often do. Resist the temptation. You *fill* the pool—after *they* build it.

TOOLBOX

Stay out of the kitchen! Until they burn the roast, let your ad people serve it up.

WANNA BUY A DUCK?

When you're in business, dozens of people want to sell you dozens of things—especially things that can be used as promotional gimmicks. Use the acid test: Will it help you sell any more of your product or service?

The answer is not always obvious, so run ideas by your ad counsel. They may have already fought—and won—this battle. And what they learned in the process could save you much-needed money.

I once served as the ad agency account supervisor for a multi-franchise auto dealership. Somebody sold the dealership on the idea of giving away a television or videocassette recorder with the purchase of a car. We waved the red flag, but to no avail—they had already decided to do it.

Two weeks later, the general manager had a room full of TVs and VCRs—and a lot full of cars.

He forgot a critical piece the of the marketing-driven ad campaign: **knowing what customers *really* want**. In this case, the ad agency had been around this block before. We knew what auto buyers would say: "I came here to buy a car. I already have a TV and a VCR. Take the $300 off the price of the car, or give me some upgrade or accessory worth $300."

The next week, when we sat down for our strategy session, the client conceded.

"Okay, you win; we made a bad call. What should we try?" he asked.

Now it was our turn. Fortunately, we had a plan, and the client was ready to listen to it. Together with the ad agency, the dealership developed a winning program—*zero percent financing and zero down.*

It was simple and actually cost nothing. Instead of giving the usual $3,000 discount off the $23,000 sticker price, they used the $3,000 to "buy down," or pay off, the interest charges on the loan. The customers saw this as a great value. In fact, they bought more aftermarket (add-on) items, since they felt they had gotten such a great deal. The dealer actually achieved both higher profit and higher volume.

Moral: *It pays to listen to competent advertising counsel.*

TOOLBOX

Your ad people need to think like your customers. Make them prove they can.

TEN YEARS AFTER

Try to imagine having a store full of great stuff people need. You've checked around, and you're sure it's priced right. You've put the word out—but they're not buying.

To find out what people need and want, sometimes you've just got to ask a local. There's no substitute for knowing what goes on in a community.

A large apartment complex in my home county decided to convert to condos. It's in a suburban area about twenty-five miles outside of New York City. The area was in a hot growth cycle. Affordable housing was scarce. The developer hired a New York ad agency to promote the sale.

- They offered free appliances. There were few takers.
- They offered lower mortgage interest rates. There were *fewer* takers.
- They offered a limited-time reduced price. And then there were *no* takers.

How could this be? The complex sits in the middle of a corporate mecca. Young singles and young families poured in for the plentiful, well-paying jobs. Rents in the area were high, while single-family homes were prohibitively costly. So affordably priced condos should sell. Right?

Wrong. Why? They misread the marketplace. Entry-level buyers (young people with solid incomes) were the primary prospects. By the time they paid their rent and their car payments they could not save anything for a down payment.

I told them to offer the condos with *no down payment*. They refused. Ten years later, "For Sale" signs still hang at the "mondo condo."

Hiring good ad people is not enough. **You have to hire someone who knows your local market.** Add some "know-where" to your "know-how," if you want to win.

IS ANYONE OUT THERE?

By now you're thinking, I get it. I need to let my ad people and my staff do their jobs. I need ad people who are both creative and analytical; I need to know what my customers really want.

But that's not all. You need some "know-when," too.

Time means money, and timing also means money. For years, a manufacturer of driveway and patio paving stone used the same advertising media—newspapers and cable TV. There was just one problem: Their products only had a ten-week selling window, during April, May, and June. When winter ends in the Northeast, the ground thaws, and so do the people. When spring comes, homeowners hit the great outdoors. It's off to the ballpark, the picnic, and the beach. Both newspaper readership and TV viewership drop like a rock.

How do you hit a moving target? Move with them! Talk to them in their cars. When we suggested they follow their customers around with morning drive radio ads, sales increased by 33 percent.

The following year, we repeated the same approach, and sales rose *an additional 50 percent!*

It literally pays to listen—especially to someone who can add some "know-when" to your advertising.

TOOLBOX

Ad agencies typically charge a 15 percent commission, which is already included in the cost of the media, so that it does not come directly out of your pocket. End the media guesswork; let *them* do the "media legwork" . . . at no additional cost to you.

WHERE HAS ALL THE TRAFFIC GONE?

You need to listen to people—but to whom, and about what? The guy or gal who lives two miles from your doorstep might know your customers even better than you do—even if he or she doesn't know your products like you do. Listen and watch.

Sometimes you have to watch the way they drive. A very successful jewelry store owner decided to open a second store near my house. Both stores were located in upper-middle-income areas. Both stores were in high-traffic strip shopping centers with supermarket anchor stores. Both stores kept the same hours. Both stores used similar advertising media. The second store should have succeeded just like the first one, but it didn't. What went wrong?

The second store sat in the westbound lane of a divided highway. But a controlled intersection made it easy to cross the highway. However, all the traffic passing by store number two went eastbound in the morning. People don't shop for jewelry on the way to work and the store did not keep evening hours. When everyone passed by on the way home, the store was closed. Within one year, it shut down.

TRAVELER'S ADVISORY

"If you build it, they will come." Will you be ready for them when they show up?

We'll assume you have the perfect ad campaign ready to go. The phones will ring, and you'll make money, right? Maybe—if there is follow-through. If your ad guys and gals are worth their salt, they'll tell you what to do *after* the ads start running.

For years, a major cruise line paid its travel agents to do mailings to their regular customers. One year, the district manager decided they should attract new customers. He arranged to spend a lot of money on a major metropolitan radio station and designated one travel agency to field the responses.

The station pulled in a huge number of phone calls. It became evident that the designated agency did not know how to turn the calls into reservations. The money and time spent on the campaign was wasted.

Advertising is one thing, but you have to train your staff—again and again.

SUCH A DEAL

It doesn't matter what you sell. Either you do the right thing and you win, or you don't, and you lose. Just remember that somebody out there knows more about what needs to be done than you do. Your job is to find that somebody. If you don't blow the wax out of your ears and pay attention after you find them, it's going to cost you. Your own product or service may not be the cheapest, but you're sure it's the best, or you wouldn't sell it. The same applies to advertising opportunities.

We were once hired by a manufacturer of nutritional supplements. They had decided to get behind a new weight-control product. Unfortunately, their hunger for savings outweighed their good judgment. It turned into their last supper.

Here are some of the considerations:

- They were relying on direct sales, via phone orders, with no retail distribution. This method involves direct-response advertising, which requires frequent repetitions.
- Against our recommendations, the advertisers ran their campaign on a small radio network promising extremely low-cost nationwide coverage.
- Weight-control products do well in warm weather where people wear less clothing, appealing to young, appearance-conscious adults. We offered them markets like Daytona Beach. They wanted markets like Buffalo.
- Lower-income people do not spend as much on weight-loss products.
- There were similar, better-known products on the market.
- They insisted on advertising in November, yet the number one New Year's resolution is to lose weight, following holiday indulgence.

They didn't listen to us. Instead, they listened to the ad salespeople from the media outlets.

Remember, your ad people work for you, not for the media. Advertising media people will want to sell you dozens of things, and you need to use experienced ad people to analyze and screen opportunities. Pay attention to their recommendations. In this case we asked ten radio stations to submit proposals for this product, and we submitted only two of them to the client.

In the end, there were no surprises—the campaign failed to meet expectations.

TOOLBOX

The only expensive ad is the one that didn't get results—no matter how much you paid for it.

THEY PROMISED MORE FOR THE MONEY

The Latin phrase *caveat emptor* means "let the buyer beware." Which, in advertising, means, "What are you really getting for your money?" Is it value-added, or is it smoke and mirrors? Ask the right questions if you want the right answers.

So be cautious when you hear, "They promised me more for my money." One advertiser told us they selected a competitor to handle their broadcast campaign because they would get 20 percent more commercials. When we asked how, they answered, "with barter."

But if you're running ads in major markets on major radio stations during the second or the fourth quarter of the year, when stations become sold out, *barter ads are the first things to get bumped.* The ads simply will not air, and the result of your bartering is 20 percent more of nothing, which is nothing. With bartering, either they were offering secondary stations in smaller markets, fringe times that stations couldn't sell, or a slow time of the year when you didn't want to air your message anyway.

Once again (and again, and again)—*listen, listen, listen.* But be careful whom you listen to. How much of this agency's business is radio buying? Who else do they buy for? What success stories can they cite?

You get what you pay for. Think of your own business. Do you give away hot-selling items during your peak season? *No!* If barter drove the ad business, nobody would be spending the billions of cash dollars that companies spend each year on advertising.

INSIDERS IN THE KNOW

One of our clients promotes concerts. When he made the mistake of letting his talent buyers negotiate with a major New York City radio station, the first half of the campaign went up in smoke. As experienced broadcasters that worked inside the station environment, we knew the inner workings of the machinery. The station had offered him a schedule at a flat rate per commercial, at the middle of the rate card, on the run-of-schedule. What's wrong with this, you ask? In May, in New York City, music radio stations very quickly hit sellout levels. When that happens, the traffic (scheduling) computer automatically bumps commercials out of prime time, unless the advertiser is paying top dollar. The result: The concert ads were all pushed into evenings and weekends—at a higher price than that time was worth. Once we pointed this out, the client turned the balance of the campaign over to us. We had the station rewrite the order, change the rates, secure a better rotation of times . . . and got the advertiser more commercials for the same money—and more ticket sales. Render unto Caesar that which is Caesar's. Hire the right folks and you'll get the right results.

WHEN IN DOUBT, ACT SMART

A close friend of mine is a sales trainer. He always told us to concentrate on high payoff activities. Figure out what high payoff activities are best for your business—setting appointments? making presentations?—then spend your time there.

Advertising builds traffic but doesn't always close deals. You need prospects. Advertising will find them and bring them to you.

Who are the smartest businesspeople you know? Chances are, they're the smartest because *they know what they don't know.* They surround themselves with people who know what they don't know. Do what they do. The world is too complicated to know and to do it all. We don't go to court ourselves, we don't do our own taxes, and most of us don't fix our own cars. We shouldn't do our own advertising either. One of my clients recognized the sad fact that he just never got around to doing his advertising—until he hired a marketing director.

Today's lesson: You don't have to have Rockefeller's money to have advertising that works. Whether you hire a one-person freelancer working from home, or a full-service ad agency, *get help!*

Ad agencies buy advertising media for many businesses; you only buy for one. Therefore, an agency's buying power may get you lower ad rates or better ad placement. Hire them, and you may get more ads for the money, or ads that get noticed more.

BRIGHT LIGHTS, SMALL TOWN

One of the really amazing things about advertisers is what they want to believe, or have grown accustomed to believing. Challenge your belief systems. One of the greatest misconceptions goes like this: "If you're not in New York/Los Angeles/Atlanta . . . your work really couldn't be any good."

Richard Bienvenue, owner and operator of Foteck, a photography studio in the Baton Rouge, Louisiana, area, is living proof of just the opposite. Most of his clientele are from outside his local area. He produces top quality catalog work for both large and small companies. How does he do it, and why does he do it?

Bienvenue uses competitively priced printers for his clients' catalogs everywhere from California to Tennessee. He flies to most of his accounts in his own small, private aircraft. "It's a tool, just like a camera—besides, I can get to the shoot and be back to my studio quicker and less expensively than on a commercial flight." Maybe that's how he turns around large signage jobs in just ten working days. But that's not all that's different about Foteck's owner.

Bienvenue refuses to move his operation to a big city, instead choosing to keep both his overhead and his wages lower. What the advertiser needs to learn, he says, is that he is saving them money while delivering them a better-quality job. Being in the right place matters.

chapter 5

Anything's Better Than Nothing, in Advertising . . . Not

In order for your advertising campaign to qualify as a campaign rather than an afterthought, your efforts must include certain elements, which we'll outline below.

The campaign must produce results. No matter what anyone tells you, advertising is first a science, secondly, an art. And since it is primarily a science, you can and should make everyone involved accountable for the results they achieve. You have a right to expect a justification for media plans and for creative concepts.

For instance, your ad people may sit down with you one day and say that what you need is a pink bunny marching across the screen beating a drum. Whatever your gut reaction, stifle it—and wait for their rationale. Who knows, it may bowl you over. (It must have done that to someone, once.)

That said, let's move on to the big picture and see what goes into the making of an ad campaign.

ANATOMY OF A CAMPAIGN

The first thing a doctor learns is anatomy. Advertising being a science, we'll do the same and explore the anatomy of a successful campaign.

(Notice the use of the word "successful"—in this field, a student has plenty of cadavers to work with.)

Visual examination shows that there are two parts to the body in question:

1. Media
2. Creative

Media is the ad space you buy in newspapers and magazines, or broadcast time you buy in TV and radio programs, etc.

In order for the media side of the equation to pull its weight, it must have two components, and you cannot succeed without both:

1. **Reach.** Example: You run your ad during the Super Bowl, and millions of people see it.
2. **Frequency.** Example: You turn on your car radio and hear the same sponsor on the morning news every day.

Creative is the effort to compose the message that is put into the media. For creative to succeed, it too must produce two things:

1. **Brand awareness.** Example: They know who you are.
2. **Brand preference.** Example: They not only *know* who you are, but they *like* who you are—and they want to do business with you.

When your campaign achieves both reach and frequency on the media side, and both brand awareness and brand preference on the creative side, it will win business for you.

Let's state this in a formula:

- Media Delivers Reach + Frequency
- Creative Delivers Brand Awareness + Brand Preference

Or, to move things off the examining table and into the real world, where you are trying to sell specific products to specific people: Right Price + Right Product + Right Time + Right Audience = Right Results.

Let's call this the *persuasion equation*. Tack this formula up in your office. The next time you run a campaign, check it against the formula. If any of these factors are missing (or weak), the campaign runs the risk of being weak. If all of these factors are present in strength, your campaign *will work*.

TOOLBOX

Say it in "bite-size" pieces. Maybe you have an attractive selling proposition, but you need to "wake it up." Sometimes it's as simple as restating the obvious—while making it sound more attractive. For instance, every health club feels their offers are great deals. My client's Gold Club was no exception: $500 a year bought you unlimited access to the facility. However, the public did not climb all over it—until we ran a commercial with copy that read: "A dollar-sixty a day won't buy you lunch in most fast food restaurants, but it *will* get you unlimited racquetball, squash, and nautilus. . . ." The phones lit up like a Christmas tree.

YEAH, BUT MY BUSINESS IS DIFFERENT

So even now you're shaking your head, silently convinced that no simple formula can embody the subtle ebbs and flows of your business. Yep, we thought as much. And we have an answer: True, everybody's business is unique—but they all operate with certain principles in common.

For instance, we all have an inventory that may be physical, or embodied in our time or expertise. We all need traffic—whether it's in the door, on the phone, or through e-mail. We all need name recognition, identity, and reputation. We all need to rise above the clutter of messages that bombard our customers and prospects. We all need to grow our market share. We all need to control our expenses. We all need to maximize our return-on-investment.

Most especially, every business needs a custom advertising strategy tailored to its situation—and to its goals. Yes, goals—remember, you're doing this for results, not because you want your ex to see your name on a billboard. For instance:

- Consider the size of your trading area. Can you expand it?
- Consider the appeal of your products and services. Can you attract different customer profiles, or just more customers like the ones you already have?
- Consider your competitors. Are they too firmly entrenched to unseat, or can you find a chink in their armor?

Below, we'll consider some common examples of business situations and goals—and the kinds of advertising that can produce the desired results.

MICRO OR MACRO?

If you sell to walk-in trade, and your customers can find similar products or services on any street corner, you have two choices: Saturate your local market or reach out beyond your local market.

How do you decide which way to go? Ask yourself this question: Will people pass by other similar businesses to get to yours?

If your merchandise mix is nothing like anyone else's; if you keep unusual hours; if your location, access, or parking is superior; if your price points are unbeatable, then *maybe* they will drive past the others to yours. Maybe. But only in that situation should you use wide-reaching media outlets.

Winner: Lotsa Little Ones

There is more than one way to win. Sometimes the tail wags the dog.

If you're convinced that your product or service is superior, but people still won't travel (remember, we operate in a convenience-based economy), find a way to open more locations without dramatically increasing your overhead. One main location can serve as a warehouse; then a series of "satellite" offices or stores, mall kiosks, or even "lease departments" (inside someone else's larger location) can give you the convenience of multiple locations. Now, you can spend the same advertising dollars in a wide-reaching advertising medium, get the increased benefit, and amortize the cost across several locations.

Okay, you made the investment in these mini-locations, you shuttle product back and forth from the main location—now what do you do? Well, you've also picked up some other advantages. You're moving more volume now, so you've got better buying power and discounts with your suppliers, and the public thinks of you as this big major player, so they figure you're the place to shop. How does that change your advertising strategy?

Here's the kicker: **You're also able to spend more, so you're a bigger player with the media.** Meanwhile, media people are competing for your business, resulting in better advertising deals. And using higher circulation media will result in higher response rates to your advertising.

Oops! Your *cost-per-response* just went down! Now you can advertise more for the same money, and drive more traffic. If your sales staff does their job, higher traffic will mean higher sales.

In advertising terms, the media side of your campaign is bigger and better. You can now advertise more prominently, and in more places. But what about your creative strategy? Does that have to change, too?

Well, yes—now you can play up the convenience of more locations in each ad, talk about how your volume means lower prices . . . and don't forget better availability and delivery/installation.

"Lone Wolf on Main Street"—Still a Winner

Suppose you're just not there yet. You sell a look-alike, sound-alike product on Main Street, and you can't expand to other locations. No one is going to walk past a competitor to get to you, although you hope they'll at least cross the street.

Face it: You're bound to a five-mile radius, and you need to dominate that area. You need to stay top-of-mind. How often do people buy your product? Are you the dry cleaner they can visit every week, or the carpet store they only see once in ten years? (Yes, *ten years*.)

The answer will tell you what to do. If you're the dry cleaner, your advertising must be consistent and omnipresent. Use media that will build frequency. At the same time, use multiple media outlets to build reach and to reinforce the message. What about creative? Your message needs to build customer loyalty and repeat business. Your prices are probably already low, and extremely sensitive to the competition's. Use "club cards" that offer discounts on the back end—for instance, one free cleaning after you buy ten.

What about the carpet guy or gal? Don't wring your hands. First, you need to find a way to bring people in more than once in ten years. Offer a free cleaning. It gets you into the home, and you can spot that worn carpet before they start shopping for a new one. Leave them a regressive discount coupon, where the amount of the savings *decreases* the longer they wait to use it.

As for media strategy, the infrequently purchased product needs what we call a "horizontal" campaign. This means light yet consistent advertising. It produces a buildup effect. When consumers come into the market for your product, they already know who you are. If your business shows spikes at key periods, add to the advertising during those times. You will heighten the effect without greatly increasing your cost.

REACH OR FREQUENCY?

As we said earlier, every business needs both. But some need more of one than the other. Remember, making your ad bigger does not proportionately increase its readership, because the number of people who can ever see it is finite. After a certain point, you're better off running your ad in more places, thereby getting the benefit of more audiences.

So which medium should you use? Once you've evaluated costs and geographic coverage, you need to dig deeper. We live in the age of "narrowcasting." No business—nor advertising medium—can be all things to all people. Consider the lifestyle and habits of the people who buy your product or service. If it's mass appeal, your choices are many.

If you want your ad to point people to your location, then consider outdoor or transit advertising. If you want to lure them away from a competitor, then land in their mailbox. If you want to reach them en route to shopping, then talk to them on their car radios.

A few years ago, I actually turned my car around and drove farther to purchase a microwave oven from an appliance discounter when I heard the sale ad. Nothing beats immediacy. (In advertising, we call it "recency," or "the proximity effect.")

If your product has a specific demographic appeal, this dictates your media choices. Consider the age, sex, income, lifestyle, and ethnicity of your customers. What media choices match your customers best?

Meanwhile, what about the customers you *don't have* yet, but want to attract?

Take a look at your competitors. Have they already oversaturated the media they use? Don't get lost in the shuffle. Look for an equally good medium they may have overlooked. Getting there first gives you an advantage.

1-800-YOU WIN

Suppose most of your business comes over the phone. Your media strategy may be entirely different from that of retail, walk-in operations.

First, if you service customers mainly by phone, you're not limited by a trading area, unless your supplier or franchiser has granted you a specific territory. The world is your oyster—with its many pearls.

Media-wise, depending on the limits of your budget, you can buy national publications, national network radio, and network television. Many of these vehicles are highly targetable. You can buy talk radio to reach more mature adults. You can buy music radio to reach a particular lifestyle—country, rock, urban—you name it. You can buy all-sports. You're selling cookware? How about TV cooking shows? You sell high-end stereo equipment? There's a magazine, or several, for that. It's a beautiful thing.

Keep in mind that direct-response, phone-order selling requires more frequency than store support does. Consumers need to see and hear the message a few more times before they react.

If your business depends on inbound phone calls, plan to spend the money you saved (by not having run to a store-front retail operation) on additional advertising. You'll need it.

Direct-response, phone-order advertising requires a whole different creative strategy, as well. Every second or every inch of the ad has to *SELL*. Throw out the rules for institutional advertising and brand-building. There is only one purpose to each and every ad you run: Sell product *NOW*. To that end, you need:

- A strong consumer benefit right up front.
- A sense of urgency—a reason to buy *now*.
- A convenient way to order, such as a toll-free number or a Web site.
- A convenient way to pay.
- A promise of quick delivery.

If your ad doesn't offer all of the above, you will fail. Don't make it pretty—just make it easy to buy.

Catalogs make it easier to order at the customer's convenience. The challenge is to get the recipients to not throw away the catalogs—in fact, to open them at all.

Catalogs originated as a way to serve people in remote areas. They continue to serve that need, along with those who just find retail shopping trips too time-consuming. Today, savvy catalog marketers don't depend on repeat purchases alone. They advertise the catalog itself. They open retail stores. They launch Web sites.

Even a special-interest catalog still needs promotion. Consider the ads for photographic products in photo magazines. Both amateur and professional photographers read these. Often, catalogs advertised in the magazines carry products not found in local retail camera stores.

TOOLBOX

When choosing media, remember, each media outlet has a finite number of readers, viewers, or listeners. You need repetition to build frequency, and different media to build reach.

CYBERSTORE?

Ten years ago, people progressive enough to see the Internet as a sales medium thought all they needed to do was put up a Web site. Many such sites came tumbling down when the orders didn't come flooding in. A couple of years later, people thought all they had to do was register with the right search engines. That's what the engineers told them to do. That didn't make anyone rich either.

Enter the marketers. Today, you can't turn on a TV or radio, open a publication, or drive past a billboard without seeing a *www.somethingorother.com* being touted.

Here's what we've learned. Look at the most successful e-commerce sites (not the ones devoted primarily to information). You'll note that these marketers know they need to *drive traffic to their sites*. Many sites have figured this out, but Amazon.com and CDNow.com found out early in the game. You must promote your Internet business *offline*, as well as online.

So ask yourself: Why are there so many "dot com" ads on the radio? The reason may not be unrelated to a *USA Today* poll that found that about two-thirds of all Web surfers are listening to the radio while they're online. A quick way to close the loop between a media exposure and a purchase? You bet! I'm checking my stocks, hear an ad for a mortgage company, and click—I'm there, checking it out. It's the age of immediate gratification, so use media with immediacy.

What about creative for offline Internet advertising? In truth, much of it is lost on baby boomers, seniors, and anyone not part of generations X and Y. The fast-moving, MTV-style commercials are missing a huge part of the most affluent and frequent online purchasers: mature adults. Take another look before you follow suit. Don't let your "dot com" turn into "dots lost."

Meanwhile, don't forget the big picture. Are you marketing to the world in the global age—or just a sliver of it? Maybe it's time to grow in a different direction *without* abandoning your traditional base of customers.

Mike and Dave run a successful catalog-based bedding factory. After opening a factory store, they expanded to online marketing. This adds traffic to their in-house call center. Later, they began adding retail stores in shopping malls. Customers who need to touch and feel the product can go in and "test-rest" a new bed. Those with a comfort level on the Web or in the mail can order from home. They advertise in local print and broadcast media to support the retail stores, and on national network radio for the catalog and Internet.

TOOLBOX

Consider buying evening and weekend radio to promote an online business. It costs less, and evenings and weekends are heavy Internet traffic periods. Adults listening to the radio while Web surfing can hear your ad and then jump right to your site and buy.

SHOW AND TELL

Remember "show and tell" time in grade school? Believe it or not, it may have prepared you for life—and business. Let's look at some more examples of small companies that have applied the persuasion equation—the formula we described earlier in this chapter, with success. You will recall, it goes like this: Right Price + Right Product + Right Time + Right Audience = Right Results. Armed with this tool, you can now "show and sell," as they did.

Home Is Wherever the Cars Are

Broadcast advertising consultant Chris Lytle calls a car "a radio on wheels." Elsewhere in this book, we describe our success story with Anchor Concrete Corporation, a manufacturer of driveway paving stones and garden wall retaining stone. They enjoyed a 33 percent sales increase in one season, followed by an *additional 50 percent* increase the next season, simply by changing their media mix from home-based newspaper and cable to in-car radio ads.

Anchor Concrete followed our recommendations—and our formula—*without even advertising a price*. The timing and the message were right—along with the audience. Anchor drove traffic right to its dealers' doorsteps by tagging their names in the commercials. One dealer experienced a 65 percent increase. Now, that's what I call "driving traffic and sales"!

Face it: Homes and cars are the engines behind the U.S. economy. The aftermarket for both continues to burgeon. Stop and think how many consumer purchases are tied to one or the other. Mr. and Mrs. Smith buy a house, then proceed to buy everything from floor coverings to wall coverings to lawn care to roofing to indoor furniture to outdoor furniture—and the list goes on. The same applies to our automobile-based economy. Cut yourself in. Spend your ad dollars to attract the dollars your customers spend. Follow them right to the point of purchase.

Eat, Work, Play—in Bite-Sized Pieces

We worked with an auto dealer offering his customers loss-leader vehicles at below cost prices in his newspaper ads. Oddly enough, people were not responding.

The public didn't care what the final price was; they were more interested in the monthly payments. Car buyers knew how much they paid for rent or mortgage, utilities, insurance, food, clothing, etc. They each had a comfort zone in their heads—how much they could afford each month for a new car. We changed the ads to show monthly payments, and traffic plus sales increased.

Are you telling your story *in your customer's terms?* Consider how they evaluate the cost of your product. Can you make it *appear* more affordable, without charging less?

Staying Alive (and Awake)

In the 1960s, Martin Himmel ran a company that bought up marginal brands of health and beauty aids. He breathed new life into them with smart advertising campaigns. As the convenience-store industry grew, it provided an outlet for road-weary travelers. These stores provided some of the first round-the-clock retailing. How perfect!

Himmel's company advertised NoDoz, an over-the-counter, fast-acting caffeine pill, on cheap, late-night radio. Voilà! Pull in to the nearest convenience store, and you can stay awake. This is a clear example of the four right elements of the persuasion equation formula—price, product, time, audience—coming together for a successful result.

Sales Are Heating Up!

Take the case of the owner of a little hardware store in a little town. What can he do to see a *dramatic increase* in customer count? How about a truckload sale of kerosene heaters during an extreme winter cold snap? By increasing his normal advertising frequency and telling the same audience he had a sale price on something they needed, Neil Pearl did just that. Once again, it's the same tested persuasion equation formula in action. It works. *Try it.*

Sometimes They Sizzle

Here's another example of a one-store retailer in a sleepy little town that refused to lie down. Surrounded by major shopping malls and discount highway stores, Classic Thyme continues to thrive and expand. It's a gourmet cooking supply store and cooking school. They hired a local cooking show host as a guest lecturer. Along with their regular mailings to their existing customers, they advertised on the cooking show. The show host gave an extra enthusiastic sell to the commercial promoting his own appearance, and the public responded by turning out in droves. Capitalize on the *momentum and influence* of a popular local celebrity with a direct tie-in to your product. He or she can be your walking, breathing advertisement.

How Do I Sell Thee? Let Me Count the Ways

We can calculate ways to make your advertising work better. We can control the message, the timing, the pricing, and the target audience. But occasionally an *unanticipated* benefit pops up.

For instance, there was a stationery supplier who decided to jump on to the Internet early in the game. They decided to drive traffic to their Web site (*www.elitescribe.com*) during the Christmas-Chanukah gift-buying season by featuring expensive writing instruments on talk radio programs.

Wisely, they made up personalized high quality pens for each talk show host. Big plus—the hosts were impressed and gave the ads an enthusiastic push. Then came the unanticipated bonus: A local retail gift shop advertised a unique item on the same radio station, a pen with a built-in flashlight. Lo and behold, people began to call the Internet advertiser and ask for the item advertised by the other store. They perceived them as the experts in fine writing instruments. They also saw them as a more convenient way to shop. Could they get the flashlight pens in time for Christmas? Yes.

Can you profit by "coat-tailing" someone else's advertising? Probably. Just be sure you have a better delivery system.

➡ Close Enough for Comfort

In the supermarket business about two-thirds of the purchasing decisions are made within the *hour* preceding the transaction. This means shoppers are in the active purchasing mindset while en route, and from the time they enter the store to the time they hit the checkout counter. Many are influenced at the point-of-purchase. Hanging tags, known as shelf-talkers, end-aisle displays, shelf-mounted coupon dispensers, ads on floors, and the "in-store radio" public address announcements all contribute to getting the consumer to either switch brands or buy additional, unplanned items. You may be able to steer consumers to make an unplanned visit, or raise their spending level if you capitalize on this phenomenon. Try to use media and messaging that will reach them immediately prior to peak purchasing times for your business.

FINAL THOUGHT

There is no single right advertising approach that fits every business. You—and your advertising counsel—have to find the ones that fit your business best. Just examine who buys your product, and how they prefer to shop. How big do you want to make your world? What motivates your customers? Are your ads playing to their needs, wishes, aspirations, travel patterns, lifestyle, and budget? Are you in front of them, in their path of travel?

Wrap the answers into a campaign with the elements we laid out, using the persuasion equation formula. Then, look for results. You'll probably get them.

◀◀ Time Capsule: "Eat at Ari's"

Okay, business owners, it's time for another trip aboard our time capsule to visit our eternal restaurant and partake of a few eternal truths—and lunch.

Skirting the chariot jam, we find it beside a big arena: Ari's, with the best gyros in urb.

Did you see those little carvings on the trees, all the way over? They said, "Best vittles this side of Carthage; fit for a king. Curb your horse." Ari's a big believer in outdoor advertising—it leads us right to his door, even if it's not slated to become a classic.

The P.A. system adds a certain touch. What's that? "Will the owner of a gold chariot with a black horse please move it? You're in the space dedicated to the appeasement of the god Apollo the Physician. And by the way, we're having a special today on burnt offerings; buy one calf, goat, or sheep, and get the second at half price."

Of course, the real drawing card appears to be the beautiful women in the togas on the front steps. But Ari doesn't stop there. He knows he can't base his business on businessmen's luncheons alone.

For instance, at the local theater they put on Greek tragedies. And the programs say "Eat at Ari's—Freshest Fish on the Mainland" on the back.

For the sports crowd, there's the arena. The billboard says, "Swords, spears, and javelin contests. Loser treats for dinner at Ari's." Ingenious, if not necessarily appetizing.

Basically, Ari seems to have a lock on this city. He leads his customers to his door with those billboards; he advertises at large crowd events; he caters to all strata of society. He uses a mixed media approach—print, broadcast, and outdoor. He's got great point-of-purchase displays. I wonder if he's advertising to those ships coming in at the port. Hey, look at those sails—very clever. **»**

The Highlight Zone: "Fighting Back"

Imagine—you picked out the best location money can buy; you have just the merchandise people want; you keep the hours customers need. You've carefully hired and trained the right people. They know your merchandise; they even know your customers.

Today, you drive to your business just as you have every day for years. You put the key in the door, turn on the lights, and greet each employee as they arrive—but something's different.

It's your customers. They're missing. You nervously retrace your steps, trying to figure out what happened. You look for interferences to your business—road construction projects, labor disputes—but there are none.

You quickly examine this week's ads. Everything is spelled right; all the prices are right. You turn on your radio, then your television. Nothing is different.

Then the mail comes—with an ad for a competing store. It's a big, bright circular with low prices. You drive over to the new place. There they are—your customers, clutching the circulars.

While you drive back to your store, you pass two men posting a billboard for the new store—right across from your business!

As you enter your empty store, it hits you—if you can promise the customers something they can't get at the new store, they'll find their way back to you.

That night, while they're watching the evening news on TV, your message crawls across the bottom of the screen:

"Bring their circulars to us, and we'll extend your warranty service."

You repeat the offer on their car radios first thing in the morning. And now the other storeowner is wondering where all the customers went.

It's a cruel twist of fate in the Highlight Zone—for someone else.

chapter 6

I Don't . . . So Nobody Does

"All my customers read/watch/listen to what I do, right?" Wrong!

Be absolutely clear on this: You and your customers do not necessarily have the same habits—especially if you're from different generations. The baby boomers are in their fifties, and their pop icons—Rod Stewart, Paul McCartney, Mick Jagger—they're all in their sixties now.

Those in their peak earning (and spending) years are not listening to the big bands and "elevator music" their parents listened to at their age. "Oldies" stations now play the Beatles and the Rolling Stones—and attract forty- to fifty-year-olds.

Today, people live longer, work longer, and remain active consumers longer. As you plan your advertising, this affects both your media choices and your creative approach. The overall demographics of the U.S. population have shifted dramatically during the past generation. There simply *is* no "average U.S. citizen" anymore. If there was, he or she would be older, more educated, possibly not a native English speaker—the list goes on.

Ask for the research—or do your own. Find out how old your current customer profile is; their education level; their habits, needs, wants, aspirations. Then, and only then, can you determine where to find more customers *like* them. What *do* they read, watch, listen to? Hold a prize drawing with a survey card, and you may be surprised to learn they are very different from you. Now, compare them to the viewer-listener-reader profiles of the advertising media you plan to use.

Just as importantly, what about the prospects you're *not* attracting? They may have an entirely different makeup.

How valuable is research to the small business? Well, I was once hired to save America's oldest country-and-western radio station from extinction. We had no budget for research. For two nights, the entire staff gathered over the sandwiches and pizza I had bought. We did a ten-question callout survey to more than 100 residents of our home county. We ascertained what programming they really wanted from their local station. And we gave it to them.

WKCW-AM had completely disappeared from the ratings for its home county in northern Virginia. But after reprogramming to the results of our survey, one rating book showed us rising from zero to draw even with our competitor across town—despite their having a full-time FM license and our having only a daytime AM license.

Find out *what* your current customers are buying now, *where* they buy it, *why* they buy it there—and most importantly, what it would take to make them *switch*. And give that to them, if doing so is within your power.

Domino's Pizza is a classic example. Any focus group could identify for you (and for Domino's) the pizza-buying public's biggest complaints: wrong orders, slow delivery, and pizzas that were cold on arrival. Then you (and Domino's) can guarantee to avoid those mistakes.

So whether you have one pizza stand or a national chain, here is what you need to do when it comes to research:

- Find the need.
- Satisfy the need.
- Deliver the promise.
- Create an "in your face"/gonzo ad campaign to get the word out.

Let's look at another example: a college dropout, Bill Gates, who became one of the richest people on earth. He generated a lot of grousing about "unfair" competition, but what did he really do? Here's *his* success formula. Use it; it will work for you, too.

- Build a better mousetrap.
- Proliferate the marketplace.
- Forge strategic alliances.

And you can do that, too. You simply have to do enough homework to find out who really buys your product, what they really care about, how to approach them, and how to motivate them.

RESEARCH THE RULES BEFORE YOU BREAK THEM

About fifteen years ago, a New Jersey radio station was sold to new owners. NJ101.5 FM broke every rule in the programming book. They put talk on the FM band; they mixed music and talk; they refused to accept the second-class status accorded to suburban stations. Instead of aligning themselves with either New York or Philadelphia, they set about carving out an identity and a mission to "superserve" New Jersey.

It worked. Today, they reach more than 700,000 adults—more than some metropolitan stations in the top 100 markets. Here's their success formula:

- Dare to be different.
- Achieve and maintain a high profile.
- Keep the momentum going.
- Use guerrilla tactics; dominate by reducing the size of the battlefield.
- Grow the demand; grow your revenues.

NJ101.5 continues to offer its listening audience constant news, traffic, and weather for its six-county service area. The station maintains brightly colored billboards year-round (not just during ratings periods). They made their mark with a brand of irreverent talk and quality news coverage that, in one breath, bashes the governor, and invites her as a guest to field listeners' calls later that same day.

They identified a problem: the lack of a strong broadcast media identity in the Garden State, which languishes in the shadows of New York and Philadelphia. By becoming a major voice of the common New Jerseyan, NJ101.5 FM attracted large audience numbers. The ratings, in turn, attracted advertisers. As demand grew, the station raised its rates (and its revenues) to levels rivaling some of its New York and Philadelphia competitors. Best of all, it eclipsed all other New Jersey stations in both revenues and ratings.

A Tale of Two Countries

Of course, you don't have to do any research. If someone did happen to do any, you can feel free to ignore it. Consider the Germans, who produced the best optics in the world (microscopes, telescopes, cameras). However, they missed the mark (and the deutschmark) by not understanding what the public wanted—and the public did not want to pay premium prices for the best optics.

The Japanese, on the other hand, provided a product that was of *acceptable* quality, priced right, and easily available. Nearly every camera purchased in the United States today was manufactured in Japan. Even Kodak is not American-made.

And let's not forget the small-car market. Volkswagen got there first, and should have owned it—not Toyota. *Banzai!*

ROYAL SCREWUPS

Keep in mind that you don't have to be a major country to achieve a royal screwup. All you have to do is ignore what works.

And that is easy to do if you listen to the wrong people. As we said in an earlier chapter, when it comes to your advertising, lots of people want to sell you lots of stuff. You and your advertising counsel have to determine what the "right stuff" is for your business.

An emerging national franchised chain of doughnut shops opened its first outlet in a new marketplace. Someone forgot that few if any consumers recognized the store name. Someone forgot that it was a stand-alone store, outside any mall or strip center. But someone at the local radio station did sell the store on having a live remote broadcast for its grand opening—without any prior advertising. What happens when no one knows the store name or location? That's right: No one came.

Compare that to our earlier success with the live broadcast at the waterbed store. Unless you have a well-loved personality, a highly motivating giveaway, and established name-product-location recognition, don't expect people to break down the doors. Because it takes a lot of doughnuts to pay for a big promotion.

READY . . . AIM . . . MISS!

Misreading either the target audience or your target medium can be just as detrimental as not completing your research. Once again, get advice from good ad people. Like our car dealer in a previous chapter, ask someone who has already driven around this block before.

For several years, I serviced a chain of plumbing and bath supply stores. For many years, they had both a consumer and a contractor following. They usually ran just one annual promotion for the public: "The Ugly Bathroom Contest." Homeowners brought in photos of a bathroom badly in need of remodeling. The ugliest entry won a gift certificate toward new fixtures.

But even though the contest proved successful, they resisted the idea of expanding their consumer advertising. One of the owners objected, saying they had analyzed their receipts and found most of their dollar volume came from the contractors.

Good point. Except that Mr. Bacciagaluppi the plumber does not wake up some morning and decide that Mrs. Thomas of Ridgewood needs a black sink with gold faucets. He buys it because *she tells him to* install one. In short, the female homeowner is actually the one who creates the demand for the product. The contractor just buys what she tells him to buy. When we pointed this out, they expanded their advertising.

And they grew from six stores to nine. So ask yourself, who is your *real* target?

For many years, home improvement advertisers believed that men bought and used their products. Maybe times have changed, or maybe these were really couples' decisions and purchases all along. The fact of the matter is that even when women are not the primary users of the product, they often influence the purchase.

Consider the backyard barbecue gas grill, typically used by the male of the household—but under the close supervision of the significant other. A wholesale distributor of barbecue gas grills once asked me whether he should run his advertising on the all-sports radio station to target a male audience. After doing a little research, I told him not to. In fact, the trade association for his industry had commissioned a survey and found that while men actually purchase the grill, and even use it more often, women are involved in the decision—including when and where to buy it.

We recommended a talk radio station with a 60 percent female and 40 percent male audience. Three years later, the distributor still advertises on that station with excellent results.

Once again, consider asking the experts. Branding consultants Fran and Bill Lytle of Bound Brook, New Jersey, have re-engineered some of America's largest companies—after their marketing trainwrecks. The Lytles conduct a series of workshops on marketing to women, to youth, to African-Americans, and to Latinos. It's worth the plane ticket. See: *www.brandchamps.com.*

SUNDAY WILL NEVER BE THE SAME

Remember the examples of the condo conversion and the jewelry store in an earlier chapter? They underscored the importance of adding some "know-when" and some "know-where" to your advertising. Here's another glaring example.

Why do auto dealers run the bulk of their advertising budgets in Sunday newspapers? There are two reasons: Their competition does, and that's what they've always done. And that's that.

We dug deeper. We found that the vast majority of people prefer to shop for a car on Saturdays. In many states, dealerships are required by law to close on Sundays—exactly when the ads came out. So the dealers were actually advertising a week ahead, hoping that customers would save or remember the ads when they shopped.

We told our client to run both his radio and his newspaper ads from Wednesday through Saturday, to build up his Saturday traffic and sales. Once again, we capitalized on the "proximity effect," taking advantage of immediacy.

➡ Add Some Know-What

Now that you know how important it is to appear in advertising media that reaches your customers, examine your advertising *message*.

Does it address the people you need to motivate to buy? Maybe not. Consider cultural, generational, and gender differences. What's important to you may be meaningless to them.

For example, World War II veterans, many of today's seniors, grew up during the Great Depression. Most of these people experienced extreme poverty, yet achieved great prosperity. They are still inclined to save and to invest and are reluctant to spend frivolously.

Tomorrow's seniors will be different. In about ten years, baby boomers will approach retirement age. They grew up in times of prosperity and consumer spending. They have a greater tolerance and threshold for debt-spending. They will react more favorably to financing offers. Remember our auto dealer's ad campaign, where the monthly payments were more important than the total price?

In 2005, the U.S. Census Bureau reported nearly 23 percent of Hispanic households had five or more people, with 80 percent of these people being under the age of forty-five. Then there are the new immigrants, largely Asian and Latino. Latinos typically have larger families, are younger than the general population, and don't own their own homes. What will you say to them? Perhaps the Lopeze's would rather buy a minivan than a sports car. Tell them what they want to hear, tell them in their native language, and they'll find you. *Comprende?*

On the other hand, the Sung family, recently emigrated from Korea, works sixty hours per week, places a high value on advanced education, and is about to buy a home. The U.S. Census Bureau reported in 2005 that Asians have the highest proportion of college graduates of any race or ethnic group in the country. Advertise a fuel-efficient compact to attract them. *Kam se ham ne da!*

TOOLBOX

Today's customers for nearly every product or service look different. Consider age, ethnic groups, and subcultures. Are you inviting them in?

BREAK THE MIRROR

So just remember—before you advertise anything anywhere, know your customer and your prospect profile. Know who they are, where they are, what they want, how they shop, and what it takes to make them switch to you. Consider:

- Are they mall shoppers?
- Do they patronize mass-merchandisers?
- Do they shop closer to home or closer to work?
- Do they buy from catalogs?
- Do they own computers?
- Are they online buyers?

Speak to them where they are, when they're receptive to your message.

And last, but not least, offer them what *they* want to buy—not what *you* want to sell.

《 Time Capsule: "Eat at Brutus's"

In our search for the eternal truths offered by restaurants, we'll push the "Rome" button on the way-back machine. Brutus, they say, dices a fine Caesar salad.

It must be up ahead somewhere—see the men carrying the boar-on-a-stick? Yummy. But we lose sight of them amid crowds of revolting peasants—revolting in a political sense, we mean. Something about the staleness of both the bread and the circuses.

There's a senator—Brutus's place must be just up ahead. But this must be a truck stop—some chariots pulled up. You know what they say about the food being gamey in those places. Well, in this case maybe you don't, but that's probably just as well.

But I could have sworn Brutus's was around here someplace. I don't see any signs. They used to hand out papyrus handbills.

Well, let's try this place. No reservations? Well, here's a shiny yellow coin with our leader's likeness. Gold? Actually, it's copper. Okay, okay, we can take a hint. We came, we saw, we didn't get a table. But we're not the ones in trouble. It's Brutus who has no advertising that speaks to the tourists and out-of-towners; nothing in other languages; nothing to point the way to his place; no sampling—well, you get the idea. »

The Highlight Zone: "Love Is Blind"

Imagine, if you will, a large bustling metropolitan city at the turn of the twenty-fifth century—the monorails, the hovercrafts, the levitating people. Among them float large screens that pulsate with images, even actual objects.

An amazing sight. But a young lady approaches us, apparently oblivious to this visually seductive advertising. Have these people grown numb to it?

As we draw nearer, we notice deafening silence. With all the flashing lights, there is not a single sound. The advertising is purely visual.

The young lady enters a store and shops, perusing the objects with a scanner. Advertisements pulse all around her, but she never reacts. Meanwhile, the silence holds.

She returns to her vehicle—and brushes her hand over the raised dots on the door. Love is blind, and so are the people who engineered a world only for the sighted—a trend traceable to the twentieth century.

We live in a world of missed opportunities—don't let yours become one of them.

chapter 7

I Tried It Once and It Didn't Work . . . I'll Never Do That Again

Did you ever buy a hamburger in a fast food restaurant, and not like it? Of course. But did you then swear off hamburgers? No—you tried another restaurant.

Likewise, somebody, somewhere, has bought a product or service similar to yours, somewhere else, and had a less-than-satisfactory experience—yet still tried *you* next time.

So how come these customers are tougher than so many businesspeople? Over the last twenty years, I have heard untold numbers of businesspeople say they tried this or that advertising medium, and it didn't work, so they'll never try it again.

Perhaps it was the timing, the placement, or the message, or all three. Perhaps there is really nothing inherently wrong with advertising your business in magazines, newspapers, radio, TV, newsletters, billboards, skywriting, whatever. Perhaps, if you tried it and it didn't work, it could be because you did something wrong. And you could be hurting your business if you don't admit that you're fallible.

And there's only one way to find out what went wrong—you've got to *try it again.*

FOCUS ON THE MESSAGE

Frankly, the problem is usually not that a particular advertising medium doesn't work, or won't work for your business. As we said before, in the wrong hands, the right tools make a mess out of the project. The answer? Hire skilled workers and give them the right tools.

You can make almost any medium produce better results—if you know how. Most of the time, it's the *offer* or the creative approach (the *message*) that didn't work, *not* the medium.

If you don't believe it, pick the medium that performed the worst, use it to offer your product or service absolutely *free*, and see what happens. Remember our success story with the restaurant chain offering one free entrée to concert ticket holders? It produced dramatic results in just *one week*.

But remember, *bad offers in good advertising media still don't pull*. If you want more customers spending more money with you, you have to give them what they want, in terms they will respond to.

But people are jaded today. "Buy one, get one," "half off," etc.—they hear that every few seconds. So if you're sure you're using the right media and speaking to the right people, it's time to put your *message* under the microscope.

Test different offers and different merchandise. Is consumer financing an issue? Remember what happened when we changed the auto dealer's ad to show monthly payments instead of the vehicle selling prices? We ran the new ad in the same newspapers as the old ads, with far better results.

Look at your ad from all angles. Does your advertising sing off-key—to the audience? Remember, a rock audience will not accept Pavarotti, no matter how good he sounds to you.

Consider the environment your ad appears in. Have you created an ad that fits? Or did you put a magazine ad on a billboard? If so, get some serious tailoring.

FEATURES VERSUS BENEFITS

Earlier in the book, I spoke about the need to offer what your customers really want and about the need to sell to them in their terms. But beyond that, does your ad copy promote features you think are important, or benefits they think are important? Also, do your words have power, or do they merge into an outpouring of clichés? Let's illustrate this concept with two different ads.

Dead

Big Bob's Pet Emporium has the largest selection of fish and aquarium supplies. We have goldfish, striped bass, baby sharks, etc. Open daily, 9 A.M. to 5 P.M., Saturdays 10 A.M. to 4 P.M., Sundays from 11 A.M. to 3 P.M. Big Bob's has books and aquarium supplies, too. Bring this ad for a 10 percent discount. Offer good weekdays only; restricted to new customers. Big Bob's Pet Emporium, 566 Highway 66, Newtown, Pennsylvania.

Deadly

Swim With The Sharks! Get the best babysitter and home security system ever—no batteries needed, no assembly required. Keep your kids off the street. This week only, sink your teeth into a new pet the whole family will love. Just 1 cent a day buys you fun and protection. Big Bob's Pet Emporium, 566 Highway 66, Newtown, Pennsylvania, opposite the mall. Call and reserve your place at our free shark care seminar: (215) 555-4567.

What's So Bad about These Ads?

Notice that the first ad reads like a laundry list of your inventory—and your inventory is of no interest to the average consumer. Save the lists for in-store fliers or mail-out catalogs.

Additionally, the first ad does not mention any *consumer benefits*— only features. People don't buy features. True, the features produce the benefits, but it is the benefits that cause them to get out their wallets.

Then there are the business hours, which are confusing, take up a lot of ad space, and are guaranteed to put the reader to sleep. Frankly, people expect you to be open during regular business hours, and will call ahead if they are worried about you being open at a specific time.

As for the street address, the ad is aimed at consumers, not letter carriers. Customers operate under the assumption that your store is a large physical object that they will catch sight of if they go down a particular road.

Now, let's look at the second ad. It sells the same merchandise, but presents it in a more attention-getting way. The tongue-in-cheek humor attracts attention. Then come the benefits: family fun and wholesome activity for kids. The registration for an in-store event will help you capture customer data for a future "warm" mailing list of people interested in aquariums and/or cold-blooded marine predators.

So, which ad would *you* respond to?

Now, look at your own ad campaigns. Are they dead, or deadly? Consider:

- Do they offer features or benefits? The first ad concentrates on features—a list of items the stores carries, its hours, etc. The second ad above emphasizes benefits—things you'll get value from if you buy the product. In this case, the benefits are: a diversion for children; a low-maintenance product; an activity for the whole family; fun, protection, and a free training session included.

- Do they get attention, or blend in with the rest?
- Do they invite customers in?
- Do they offer an enticing incentive to drop in?

Homework

Create a dead ad and a deadly ad. Run both in the same advertising medium just a few weeks apart. What results do you get? You may want to go back and try that advertising medium again—the one you said you'd never try again.

But don't stop there. Go back and review every ad you've ever created for your business, whether it was a "help wanted" ad, a grand opening ad, an anniversary ad, a new product or service introduction—whatever. Look for what was missing.

Now, re-create the ad that would help your business most at this very moment—and place it in the same medium you were convinced would never work for you. Monitor your results; then, run the same ad in other media. Compare your results.

Remember, you tried it once, and you *need* to try it again. Just do it better this time.

REVISING HISTORY

Of course, sometimes the mistake is to consider doing something other than what you've been doing all along. For instance, a long-time radio colleague of mine referred me to an auto dealer friend of his. The dealership had been on the local radio stations for years. They simply did not know whether the advertising continued to pull for them.

So we devised a campaign entitled the "History of Wheels." Each new episode had historical characters from various periods—the fictional "ancestors" of the dealer—solving the transportation problems of the era. Not only did the store owners and employees hear constant comments on the theme—from the golf course to the doctor's office—but people wanted to know what would come next.

Obviously, the advertising was still pulling. And we were able to learn that because we tried something new.

Remember when we dramatized the intensified effect of the persuasion equation formula when used by a local hardware store? During an extreme cold snap, they ran a truckload sale of kerosene heaters. We increased the frequency of the ads, placed a deadline on the sale—and the store reported results *ten times* higher than the normal customer reaction. But they were still *using the same advertising medium,* just in a different way.

TOOLBOX

Consider: If your ad campaign included an instruction manual, would you read it? Most people probably wouldn't. Consider this book as the "owner's manual" to each and every ad campaign you run. Check them against the instructions I've given you, and you'll succeed.

PUSH THE ENVELOPE

Then, there are the times when specific problems may demand specific solutions—solutions that might never come to mind under the heading of "advertising." The mistake in such cases is to reject the idea out of hand because it sounds so different.

Take the case of Harry & Irv, who had a great business concept. Long before hordes of "odd lot" chain stores came along, these two liquidators bought up quality, name-brand men's and women's apparel from retailers going out of business. They sold them in a warehouse-type store with pipe racks and a "no frills" environment. Even with an excellent jingle, and a good schedule of both radio and newspaper ads in the strongest local media, the public only trickled in.

What was the problem? After all, the store had a unique concept for the time and was only one block from the hottest corner in town. However, it was *out of the line of sight of that corner,* down a hill, on a side street.

So we paid a part-time actress to dress up as a mime, stand in the town square, hand out fliers, and point the way to the Bank Street Wearhouse. The traffic count increased quickly and dramatically.

If there's a lesson to this chapter, it's that any advertising medium can be made to work—but you may have to work *at* it. But if you have a worthwhile message, the results should be worth it.

◀◀ Time Capsule: "Eat at Big Charlie's"

We'll need shields and jeweled swords to blend in with the locals on this trip, as we fire up the way-back machine for our continuing tour of eternal restaurants and the advertising lessons they offer.

See that village off in the distance, with the smoke rising above the stone cottages? That's where we'll find Big Charlie's Place.

At least, I think so. I tried like hell to get him to take space on those trees during my last visit, but he insisted on putting up the whole menu . . . too hard to read on horseback. The colors were great, but the campaign tanked. Let's ask that party of men with the crossbows for directions. "We-are-hun-gry. Which-way-to-Char-le-magne's?"

Thanks guys; now, there's a unique promotional campaign. Did you see the markings on those arrows? All we have to do is follow the trail of arrows to Big Charlie's Place. Anyone here read medieval French? I didn't think so. I told him to get those things translated. . . .

Following the road with the broken arrows we find—troubadours! They're singing:

"Lend me your ears and I'll sing unto thee,

A song of a damsel so fair.

Throw us some coins and we'll sing you some more.

Meanwhile, Big Charlie's Place has the best food in town,

The others will give you the runs."

I like it. Hey, this could be the first jingle ever written. But we need to ask them, what happened to those people rolling on the ground over there? I see—they came at closing time, when the kill wasn't fresh anymore? I've got to get Charlie to start putting his hours in those ads. It could really impact his repeat business. Meanwhile, I see that Big Charlie doesn't have time to see us. Maybe after the Crusades? See you then. For now, let's walk slowly and naturally back to our time machine, without startling anyone who's armed.

Without question, these guys know how to work the hospitality game. They seem to keep the people coming back, even with an occasional mishap or two. They need to work on their language skills a little, reach out and be more proactive. They've got a good feel for choosing media, but they need to work on the message a little—you know, "sell the sizzle" a little more. Overall, they seem willing to take a little (ahem) loss here or there, to keep customers for the long haul. The singing commercial was a really nice touch. **»**

The Highlight Zone: "Never Say Never"

Imagine if you will, a business very much like your own. The owner, Mrs. Marian Grimsby, has invested the better part of her adult life in this business. Every day, for over forty years, Mrs. Grimsby has arrived at her antique shop at precisely the same time, and opened it exactly the same way.

Today, however, something's different. She's forgotten her morning dusting and is staring out the display window. Because, on the sidewalk, people are walking past the shop as if it didn't exist. Not one of them stops to wave, to nod, or to even glance at the objects in the window.

Mrs. Grimsby frets and sighs, looks again—and drops the feather duster in astonishment, because there's a new antique shop directly across the street.

Composing herself, she insists she must be mistaken. But it's still there.

She picks up the daily newspaper, looking for her ad. All she can find is the ad for the new competitor.

Finally, someone walks in—a young woman. But she's not a customer. In fact, she's selling magazine ads. Mrs. Grimsby snorts. She tried that once, forty years ago, when the store first opened, and no one came in. And she swore she'd never try that again.

But now there's competition. So she decides to try it again, this once.

A week later, on the same street, Marian Grimsby has a store full of customers. But that day a week ago was not a bad dream. As it happens, the magazine had decided to do a feature story on decorating with antiques, and her ad was there with the story. Fortunately, Marian Grimsby learned never to say never—before it was too late.

chapter 8

Why Bother? I Can't Outspend My Competition, Anyway

In the Pocono Mountains of Pennsylvania, a man with a long gray beard and little rectangular glasses shuffles across the floor of his used car dealership.

One hundred-sixty late-model vehicles grace the lot—and that many leave each month. Yes, Ralph Vecchio's Colonial Used Auto Sales enjoys total inventory turnover.

Ralph's ads appear in every area newspaper and air on every local radio station. He spends four times what his competitors spend on advertising, and he sells four times their volume. By capturing virtually his whole market's eyes and ears, he has created a sort of omnipresence, resulting in top-of-mind awareness. Nearly every used-car buyer in the region shops at his store first.

He has a fortress built out of advertising. But does that mean that you, a prospective competitor, are in a hopeless position?

No. Admittedly, there are situations, like this one, where you are probably not going to be able to outspend the competition. But so what? The key always is to *advertise smarter*, not more. Here are some proven ways to do just that.

USE MEDIA YOUR COMPETITORS AREN'T USING

Even if your competitors buy up full-page, full-color newspaper ads, you can still capture your market. If you find a medium where they don't advertise, those consumers will only see and hear you. In this way, you can dominate.

"To Boldly Go Where None Have Gone Before."

These advertisers fled the pack for the open fields—and succeeded:

Harmon Drugs, a chain of stores selling deep discount drugs and health and beauty aids, went up against national competitors that blanketed homes with full-color mail-out circulars. We fought back with a showing of brightly colored, bold billboards that remained visible long after the circulars hit the dumpster. One billboard loomed right over a competitor's store. Harmon got a big, quick response.

Schlott Realtors, a large regional residential real-estate brokerage firm competed with the well-entrenched number-one broker, as well as several nationally advertised franchises. While all the major competitors continued the tired practice of running double-truck newspaper ads (a two-page spread), Schlott's ad agency created a "TV Showcase of Homes." This Sunday morning televised "virtual walk-through" of homes differentiated the broker and its offerings from the rest. Coldwell Banker eventually acquired Schlott.

Cargo Logistics, an airport-area trucking and warehouse company, surprised people when it decided to advertise on an easy listening contemporary music radio station. What's *that* about? The station had heavy in-office listenership. When bosses told secretaries to "ship it out," they called Joan, the real secretary in the radio ads, who joked about her "two-minute lunches." When you're the only one they hear, you get the calls!

CREATE MORE MEMORABLE, ATTENTION-GETTING ADS

No matter how much they spend, how often they advertise, or how prominent their ads are, if you execute a campaign that is better at getting people's attention and at customer retention, you will succeed.

Below are some examples of campaigns that really took hold. Pay attention to the techniques that worked for these advertisers—they did not start out as dominant category leaders.

> **Honda of Mineola.** "What's a Mineola?" you ask. For years, unless you lived in Long Island, New York, you wouldn't know. Thanks to an enterprising auto dealer, the rest of New York, New Jersey, and Connecticut soon found out. After running an extremely catchy jingle on several of New York City's top radio stations, consumers were walking around singing it in offices, at ballparks, at beaches—and right into the showroom. Try and do that in the Sunday paper. It pays to grab 'em and hold 'em.

> **P.C. Richard.** The great shakeout in the consumer appliance and electronics business has long since passed. Many once-familiar chain stores have come and gone. One that remains in the New York area is P.C. Richard, which uses a simple mnemonic device to open every single radio and TV commercial. The whistling of a few musical notes establishes the store's identity in the first five seconds of every ad. P.C. has staying power—and it beats whistling Dixie!

> **Motel 6** wasn't exactly the type of place you'd want to write home about on their stationery—until Dallas ad agency the

Richards Group created their homespun Tom Bodette character. The ads poke fun at more expensive national chains, citing Motel 6's emphasis on basic comforts over costly amenities. The ads invite guests in, with the consistently hospitable tag line, "We'll leave the light on for you."

Taco Bell. Fast food is the arena of the most competitive product wars and highest spending in the ad industry. And in that arena, Taco Bell is not at the top of the (ahem) food chain. However, the continuing appearance of a Chihuahua in its ads created instant identification. Each ad in the campaign stands alone—yet ties the series together. Did anyone ever confuse this dog as a spokesperson for a hamburger restaurant? Absolutely not—and that's why people are sitting up and begging for more.

Ask Yourself:

What made these ads so successful? What did they have that's missing from most locally produced ad campaigns? Whatever it is, you need it, because the sheer weight of your media buys—how *much* advertising you buy—by itself can never be enough to make your ads rise above the clutter of the 2,000 impressions bombarding your prospective customers each day.

The Answer:

Superior creative—a better message and a better presentation of that message. But wit alone is not enough—you have to have a message consumers *want* to see and hear, and execute it in a way that makes it both *noticeable and memorable.*

How do we do that? Pay attention; learn from the best. You can build the same success elements into *your* campaigns. Here's what they do:

Find out what customers really need and want, before creating the campaign. Determine which product or service they prefer, how much they will pay, what offers interest them, etc.

Determine an approach that speaks to that consumer, in his or her own language. If they're middle-aged or above, for example, they may be alienated from a fast-moving, impersonal electronic world. Perhaps a nostalgic approach will appeal to them. If they are generation X-ers on their way up, you need to appeal to their desires for both *fun and power.* Get the hint? *Lifestage* determines *lifestyle.*

Emotion doesn't cost a nickel more. The ad must appeal to both the prospect's logical *and* emotional needs. Too often, local advertisers ignore the affective, or emotional component, of the ad campaign.

TOOLBOX

Peter Caroline, trading as Write on Target, a national award-winning freelance copywriter in Green Valley, Arizona, points out, "You cannot bore people into buying something." Peter advises against the long letters so many advertisers insist on mailing. Respect your prospects' attention spans, he warns.

We ran a series of radio ads each year for a high-end retail jewelry store chain. Their competitors ran on the same radio station. However, their stores bore no resemblance to one another. We needed to differentiate our client's five-generation-old establishment from the competing store chain. So we crafted a series of messages, each voiced by a middle-aged British "couple." Their fine, impeccable speech patterns communicated the stores' quality; the reading aloud of their gift tags struck emotional chords in the audience. We even commissioned a composer to write a classical music background to heighten the effect.

Best of all, the approach stood out so much that customers commented on it when they visited the stores.

ASK FOR THE ORDER

Too much of today's advertising leaves consumers cold. They don't come away with a clear brand perception, and often can't even identify who the advertiser was.

Worse yet, they don't know what the advertiser wants them to do—feel good about the advertiser? Feel good about themselves? Buy something, somewhere? Feed the Chihuahua?

Finally, and worst of all, the *benefits of responding* are unclear. What will I gain if I go here, click there, call there? When you see a Kodak or a Hallmark ad, it reaches you at the emotional level; it resonates with your most treasured experiences and clearly motivates you to make a purchase. Your advertising must tell your audience what you want them to buy, what they will gain from purchasing it, and how or where to buy it easily.

CREATE A BETTER VALUE PERCEPTION

No matter how much the competition advertises, if people feel your offer is better, they will gravitate to you.

But creating a better value perception does not necessarily mean underpricing everyone else. In particular, if you sell a look-alike, sound-alike product, adding and communicating value becomes extremely important. A Pontiac is a Pontiac is a Pontiac. However, if yours is delivered to the door of a busy working person, picked up for service, and dropped back at the doorstep, someone might even pay *more* for it. What can you add to your product or service that the *customer perceives as valuable*, even if it doesn't cost *you* much?

Often, advertisers are too intent on testing each advertising medium. They fail to realize it was their *offer* that failed, not the media.

A smaller ad with an attractive savings or *value enhancement* will out-pull a larger, more expensive ad.

For example, we published long, narrow "strip" new car ads that ran the full depth of the page, but only two columns wide. A price set in large type dominated, with a single featured vehicle. The resulting traffic far exceeded what we normally got from a traditional ad with a page full of vehicles.

What constitutes a better offer? Once again, *ask your customers*. Are they seniors on fixed incomes looking for the "early bird" special, or are they well-heeled retirees treating their visiting families to a memorable dinner?

What about discounting? If your goal is simply to *introduce* first-time patrons to a superior shopping experience, a "loss-leader" approach works. Otherwise, it results in cherry-picking—they'll only return when the deal is right. Conversely, if you're looking to create a *customer,* rather than just a sale, advertise other intrinsic—possibly intangible—benefits of the product.

For instance, our client's Therapeutic Pain Rub had properties that were superior to the leading topical analgesics. Its homeopathic formula worked without any of the undesirable side effects. It didn't burn, smell, stain, or stick to clothing. However, it was far less well known and was not as readily available in stores. It also cost more than the drugstore alternative. But we knew that the product had a high satisfaction level, and that if someone tried it just once we had generated a customer, not just a sale.

So we placed radio ads on an alternative medicine program hosted by a highly credible physician. He read the testimonials *other practitioners* and patients had sent to the company. This resulted in new *users* for the product. Their repeat sales and resultant word-of-mouth referrals paid for the ads over time.

In an earlier chapter, we told you that perception equals reality to the consumer. But can you make people believe your prices—and values—are better, without even naming a price?

New York City area electronics retailer Crazy Eddie did just that. He hired popular New York disc jockey Jerry Carroll to wildly gesture and crow about his "insane" prices. For years, he never stated a single price in any of the radio or TV ads that built his identity as a price leader and drove hordes of people to his stores. If they *believe* you have better values, they will come.

TOOLBOX

"The rules are the same everywhere, but people respond to different approaches in different places," cautions Steve Ong, a Los Angeles, California, writer with international experience. Steve relates, "Easterners respond more to promotional approaches; you can't 'push it' as hard on the West Coast."

DEVELOP A SUPERIOR PRODUCT POSITION

Let me illustrate this concept with an example. Years ago, I drove down a street in my state capital. I passed the familiar billboard for Honda motorcycles. It read, "Honda—Follow the Leader." A few weeks later, I drove past the same billboard. Another board had just been put up next to it. It read, "Yamaha—Follow No One."

How you position yourself against the competition can determine whether your campaign succeeds or fails. You and your advertising counsel must take a careful inventory of your strengths and weaknesses, and compare them to those of your competitors. When you focus on a single attribute of your product, service, or establishment and compare its strength to your competitors, price considerations often disappear for the consumer.

For example, Bounty paper towels are touted as "The Quicker Picker-Upper." Superior absorption outweighs cost for many consumers, who believe that they will actually *use fewer towels* when buying a brand that absorbs better. As a result, they are willing to pay *more* for the product.

McDonald's succeeds in raising the average amount of each transaction by selling "Extra Value Meals." The consumer accepts the proposition that bundling these items together costs less than ordering them individually from the menu.

The trick to creating good value perceptions involves offering something the consumer knows he or she would have to pay much more for—even if it doesn't cost you much more to offer it.

Other examples of the use of value perception:

- New Jersey clothing discounter Daffy Dan's sells "Clothing Bargains for Millionaires." It's not just a slogan. It communicates *quality and cost savings together*—and that's exactly what value is.

- Timex sold millions of watches by proving their *durability* in their famous ad campaign. Divers jumped off cliffs wearing the watch; they strapped it to the blade of a spinning outboard motor, etc. "And the Timex watch is still ticking." Why did this approach work? The public already knew Timex was priced competitively. The advertising communicated that the watch would *perform* and *outlast* others for the same money—a great value perception.

- Bergenfield, New Jersey, Ford dealer Ed Mullane delivered his own gravel-voiced radio commercials for years. He invited customers to his "bare-bones" tiny cinder-block showroom, "where we pass the savings on to you." The approach flew in the face of his larger competitors. "Because we buy in volume, we'll save you money," they kept saying. But in time, the public came to know that all dealers pay the same price for their inventory—but at the other places the customers were helping to pay for thick carpets and crystal chandeliers.

- A furniture store in Philadelphia blanketed radio, television, newspapers, and billboards with their ad: "Look for the big blue balloon in the sky; look for the big savings at the furniture store." Across town, another furniture store watched closely, and as the campaign came to a close ran its own message: "Look for the *bigger* blue balloon in the sky."

- Domino's pizza flattened the competition with an ad campaign instructing consumers to tear the competitors' ads out of the phone book and bring them in to get a discount. This meant they were offering at least the same value as their competitors. It also meant that next time these people went to their phone books to order a pizza, only Domino's ads remained. It proved to be a great way to achieve and maintain the top-of-mind position with customers.

The "Write" Fit

Maybe it was the spectacular sunset over the mesa that lured Bostonian Peter Caroline to settle in Arizona. More likely, some ghostly presence from the old West spoke to the award-winning agency copywriter. You see, Peter Caroline, who trades as Write on Target, is a firearms enthusiast who traded both the city and the big agency to cut loose and write about what he knows best—outdoor sports like hunting and fishing. To his credit, his clients followed him, sagebrush, rattlers, and all.

In Peter's words, "The smaller the advertiser, the better you can target": which doesn't mean spending more money. Caroline created fliers for a small gun shop. Fliers were stuffed under the windshield wipers of cars at gun shows, and in shooting-range parking lots, achieving good response rates.

Sometimes it means spending the advertisers' media dollars in a more imaginative, attention-getting format. Caroline cites his work for U.S. Repeating Arms Co. of New Haven, Connecticut. "The client wanted a more attention-getting format; a spread was too expensive, and many readers skip over spreads. We came up with a 'half page' spread—two facing lower pages. It was a perfect shape for portraying rifles and shotguns; there was no room for other ads on the two pages, so the top halves of both pages consisted of editorial material."

TOOLBOX

Exploit your strength . . . whatever it is. Boston's prominent Provident Bank was perceived as a large, monolithic institution. Ad agency Humphrey, Browning and McDougall turned around the negative by making their client's size work for them. The new campaign became "Put our strength to work for you."

MAKE LEMONADE, EVEN IF IT FREEZES

When life hands you lemons, make lemonade. You've heard that one. But when positioning your product, you may have to take that adage one step further. You may need to go on making lemonade even when it freezes, especially when competing against time and weather.

I once walked into a ski shop during a winter with no snow. It was fifty degrees in February. The last person the owner wanted to see was an advertising person. I held up my hands, as if to stop his protest.

I asked him, "Would you buy advertising on my radio station if your ad would run when and only when it snowed, and the snow stuck to the ground? Would you buy this advertising if you would be billed only for what actually ran, and have to pay only for what actually ran?"

Mr. Lang's answer was a resounding "YES." The next week it snowed—and his ad was on the air first thing in the morning, well before his competitors could react. And it ran while everyone was glued to their local radio station for traffic reports, weather reports, and school and business closings.

Years later, I repeated the same success story for a hardware store carrying ice scrapers, rock salt, traction sand, and snow blowers. Gleyn

Ward, National Sales Manager of KDKA in Pittsburgh, Pennsylvania, reports a similar success strategy for several of his advertisers. "A home heating oil company uses a temperature trigger. When it drops below the agreed-upon temperature, the ads run. A boot company does the same thing with snow," he said.

At this writing, we're planning a similar "sneak attack" for a manufacturer of rainwear. This is no-risk, opportunistic advertising. You can do it, too—without big budgets.

PLAN, THEN BUILD

When you're at a budget disadvantage, launching an all-out frontal assault is obviously not the way to go. The idea is to feel your way along, to establish a beachhead and carefully move inland.

Here's how you attract and retain customers:

Cast a wide net. If you're not sure who your customers really are, advertise to a general, mass audience. See who shows up. Start contests (drawings and other giveaways that they have to sign up for) to build mailing lists—do whatever it takes to achieve some measure of data capture. See who patronizes you.

Next, market to the heavy users. See which geographic and demographic group responded most. Now, step up efforts aimed directly at them. Find the media that appeals to them and tailor a message that addresses them directly.

Get to know your customers better. Find out where they eat dinner, where they get their cars repaired, where they get their hair done, etc. Then, work on cross-promotions with local, non-competitive businesses. Have them offer incentives for their customers to patronize you, and do the same for them. We introduced our client, Therapeutic Pain Rub, to another advertiser, ABED.COM. Both products, an herbal pain rub and a foam mattress, although seemingly different, work on the principle of improving blood flow. We recommended that each company include a "stuffer" for the other's product in deliveries and mailings—*at no additional cost to either one.*

Keep your existing customers. It costs four times as much to get a new customer as it does to keep an existing one. New or old, 80 percent of your business will come from 20 percent of your customers. Keep in touch with them. Have a private sale; send them a newsletter; e-mail them. Don't assume that because they're your customers today they will be your customers tomorrow.

For many years, auto dealers had customer loyalty that spanned generations. You bought your car at the same dealership where your father bought his car. Times changed. Consumers became more price-conscious as cars became more expensive. Their loyalty eroded. Many dealers were slow to change. They shook their heads in dismay when they bumped into former customers driving new vehicles purchased from competitors.

Of course, the customer had not *heard* from the dealer in the last five years, since they bought their last car. So why should they come back?

Today's smarter dealers embrace more successful strategies. For example, why not include a coupon book full of service specials with every new (or used) vehicle that leaves the lot? Once they form the service habit, the customers not only come to trust you, but when repairs become too costly, your dealership has the first shot at selling them a new vehicle. Conversely, if you can attract motorists who bought their cars elsewhere to come to you for service, in time you stand to sell them their next vehicle. (And to think there was a time when dealers resisted the idea of servicing cars that were bought elsewhere.)

Steal your competition's customers . . . in a nice way. Entice them to try you, and give them reasons to stay loyal to you.

TODAY'S LESSON

So, let me get this straight. You want me to figure out what really makes my business unique and special, how we do what we do differently and better.

Then, you want me to lay my competition on its ear by positioning my strengths against their weaknesses, right?

So far, so good.

Then, when I'm done doing this positioning thing, you want me to create a killer ad campaign to tell the world why they should call, stop in, click on, and order my stuff, right?

While I'm doing this, you want me to be sure that I'm approaching my best possible prospects—the heavy users of my product or service—and telling them exactly what they want to hear, right?

No wonder you recommended I get some help with my advertising. It's kind of like playing Ping-Pong with lots of balls coming at you, and only one paddle.

It can be done. Oh, and don't forget to make sure and appeal to both the emotional and the logical sides of your customers' brains. Did I forget anything?

◀◀ Time Capsule: "Eat at Lucreztia's"

Here in the heavily publicized Renaissance we'll see what lessons can be drawn from our eternal restaurant. It's a place owned by the Borgia family.

The word-of-mouth on the food is very negative. They put out a real nice spread, but there's always somebody who doesn't quite make it to the end of the evening. Be careful not to step on them. But if they like you, you get invited back for a second try. Come to think of it, I don't know anyone who's ever been there more than three times. Just watch out for Lucreztia's ring, they say.

It seems to me they've got prestige, décor, and a diverse menu on their side. However, they're up against a reputation for bad service. So, gang, how can we position them better?

"Where Renaissance royalty is just dying to dine?" That has promise. But we still need to overcome those negatives.

"Longest banquet table between Tuscany and Sicily?" Yeah, that's better.

Now, let's talk about some media outlets, where we can get the word out about the "new" Borgia's. We could sponsor an art exhibit—do you think that new guy, Michelangelo, would pull a crowd? We could pass out—I mean, send out—reproductions of the works, you know, just to the titled nobility. If we keep it by invitation only, we can keep out the riff-raff.

How about this? "Borgia's Old World dining, a royal tradition for generations, invites you to sample its new banquet. Come join Lucreztia and the whole family for the unveiling of Mike A's new murals—quality worthy of the Sistine Chapel."

Now, we're talking. We're only inviting people who can afford the place; we're appealing to their artistic sense, and we're comparing the food to great works of art. By positioning Borgia's with the Church, we've got morality on our side. Presto! Bye-bye, bad reputation.

Okay, let's go pitch it to the Borgias. But let's try to finish before they start pouring the wine—just in case. **»**

The Highlight Zone: "A Word from Our Sponsor"

Imagine, if you will, a blank television screen. A picture forms, and gradually you recognize the outlines of human beings. At least, we think they are. Because you're entering a dimension of sights that mean nothing to you and words you can't understand.

Strange? Maybe not. Consider the commercials that flash across your television screen every day. Notice the surreal images, the leaps from one subject to another, the brief flashes. Can you remember who the sponsor was? Did they tell you a story? What did they want you to do?

But perhaps the fault was not in the commercials. Perhaps they were simply aimed at someone else.

We live in a world that changes with each flash of lightning. Soon, we will have whole generations that speak different languages. Imagine each channel on your television set carrying a different version of every commercial: one for children, one for teens, one for young adults, one for the middle-aged, and one for seniors.

Far-fetched? Not really. Examine your advertising, and the people who create it. Are they speaking to your world, or are they from the Highlight Zone?

chapter 9

Who Needs It? I'm the Leader . . . Hands Down

Success does not breed success—it breeds complacency. And the complacent are likely to forget that leaders have to advertise to keep their lead. You see, once you become the leader, there's only one way to go . . . and that's down.

Assuming you followed my advice and as a result are now the leader, *advertise your leadership*. And while you're at it, boast about everything that *made* you the leader. The result will be a winning identity that will continue to attract customers. People assume you must know what you are doing if you *became* the leader.

Today, people and companies become business leaders in different ways—often, through mergers and acquisitions, rather than a superior staff, or through better processes, better merchandise, better levels of service, etc. But the result remains the same. Your leadership position still feeds the customer's perception of your superiority.

IT WORKS ON MADISON AVENUE

Look around you, and you'll see that category leaders keep advertising to keep their lead. Consider a trifling example: McDonald's. Does this company ever stop promoting? While far and away the undisputed leader in fast food, it never stops aggressively seeking your business. It's no coincidence that the number two player in the industry is light-years behind—and has never been able to create an ad campaign that substantially increased its market share.

Now, name the category leaders in these major industries: telecommunications, computers, automobiles, and soft drinks. The answer: AT&T, IBM, Microsoft, Toyota, General Motors, and Coca-Cola. And not only do they lead their industries; they also rank among the largest advertisers. By continuing to advertise, these companies continue to feed the public's perception of their dominance—*and the people keep buying.*

It Works on Main Street, Too

Your small business is no different. Whether you operate a retail store, cleaning service, computer repair shop, or office furniture showroom, you have a brand identity to promote.

Consider: Would you drive a *Murray?* No? Why not? For all you know, it might be as comfortable and reliable as a Cadillac. But it has *no brand identity*; therefore, it has *no value perception.*

Americans buy brands they know and trust—no matter how small or large the purchase. Treat your product, service, or establishment as a brand; build its brand equity in the consumer's mind, and you'll build brand preference. Build brand preference, and you'll build your sales volume. Build your sales volume, and you'll rise to the top. Continue promoting, and you'll stay on top.

In your trading community—whether it's online, over the phone, drive-by, or walk-in—your brand occupies a position in your potential customers' mind. As the perceived category leader, you occupy the *top* spot—for now, anyway. How much is it worth to your business to *stay* there? To the leader, continuing to advertise is yet another form of "sales insurance."

Shortly after the turn of the twentieth century, Henry Ford led the charge of the new fledgling automobile industry. His mass-production of affordable cars filled the needs of the newly mobile public.

His superior assembly-line process put him way out in front. Did he stop advertising? Certainly not.

Do not rest on your laurels. All it took was a larger, slightly under-priced Mars candy bar to unseat the Hershey Chocolate Company's leadership. Hershey's did not aggressively promote, and Mars beat them right off the shelf with a better value perception.

When your advertising becomes invisible, so does your business. Pulling the plug is the quickest way to fade from memory—and leave your enterprise unprotected to an assault. Keep advertising, and you'll keep your market share—and your lead. Keep in mind the parable of the hot dog stand.

An immigrant came to America from his native Greece. He set up a small hot dog wagon. People liked his product and his service, and continued to patronize him. In time, Demetrios's business grew. The hot dog cart became a hot dog stand, then a bigger stand. Billboards led the way: "Ten miles to Demetrios's Hot Dogs"; "Five miles"; "One mile"; "Here it is!"

Eventually, Demetrios wanted to retire. His son would soon take over the business. One day, his son approached him.

"Dad, don't you know there's a recession going on?" said the son. "Why are you spending all of this money on advertising? Take the signs down."

Demetrios figured his son had more education than he did; he must know something. He stopped the advertising. Business ground to a halt. He said to his son, "Son, you're right. There *is* a recession."

TOOLBOX

Every business is number one at *something*. Establish leader-ship; then, promote yourself as a leader. Customers will gravi-tate to you.

TUMBLING DOWN?

Unfortunately, when you reach the top, there is only one way to go: down. As the leader in your business community or product category, you stand to lose market share to competitors. They, on the other hand, stand to gain.

Unless there is a huge influx of new customers coming into the marketplace, you are fighting to *maintain* your share of the pie. However, as the volume leader, when you spend the same advertising dollars as they do, it represents a smaller share of your total sales.

On the other hand, leaders often get caught up in issues of size. When the company gets too big, it can't react quickly enough. A small competitor with a superior process or product begins to cut into the big company's market share.

Traditional, large corporate thinking says, "Throw some money at the problem." This is unnecessary. Today, in a world of faxes, modems, and overnight express, the ability to react quickly becomes more important than money.

Let me illustrate. In times of affluence, customers are more interested in, "How fast can you deliver and/or install?" than, "How much does it cost?" The same principles apply to advertising. How quickly can you react to a competitor's offer? It may be more important than how much you can spend to advertise your product. Elections are often won and lost on this principle.

In our electronic world, getting to market *first* often translates into leadership. Once you have released your product with a proper ad campaign, you can begin building brand identity and sales volume. And at that point you are light-years ahead of any competitor. Even with deeper advertising pockets, it will take some doing for them to catch up with you. Notice that knock-off products seldom eclipse the original.

Today, we are redefining leadership. Your advertising media choices must give you the flexibility to change your message quickly.

Your advertising message must be both proactive (set the pace in going out after customers), and reactive (responsive to the curve balls the marketplace throws your way.)

To do this, a company may have to reinvent itself. An example of self reinvention would be the Brunswick Corporation of Illinois. If you glanced at one of their old annual reports, you would find everything from medical products to defense contracting to outboard motors. Obviously, they had embraced the theory and practice of diversification as a means of recession-proofing themselves—even if there was no efficient way to market the resulting hodgepodge of products. Partly for that reason, the diversification approach is now considered obsolete. Today's Brunswick concentrates solely on its core business of recreational products. Today, expansion involves line extensions of *related* items. Camping stoves, tents, boating, and bowling keep the company focused on family fun—a much more marketable product mix.

GROW A CONSCIENCE

Okay, so now you're the leader in your market segment, category, town, etc. You're not complacent. You're continuing to promote your business as if its future depends on it, because you know that it does.

And now let's change gears, because it's time to consider a point they may not have made in business class, but which is a daily concern in the marketing arena.

The point is that people expect leaders to lead the community at large, not just the business community. Do not disappoint them. If you do, someone else may fill your shoes.

With the crisis in confidence in government and large corporations, we, the entrepreneurs, have the greatest opportunity of all time to lead. Use it. Take up the torch, and tell the world in your advertising. Corporate America does it with the Olympics; we do it with local charities.

The point of this sermon is that, when you are the leader, your advertising needs to "grow a conscience." What do I mean by that? Leaders are good citizens; business leaders live to serve. Paul J. Meyer of Waco, Texas, founded Leadership Management International, one of the largest training companies in the world. At age twenty-seven, he had already become a millionaire by selling life insurance. He then set about sharing the techniques that worked for him. What made him a success? Meyer's advice today remains, "Develop a servant's heart." There is no higher value than to truly *serve* your customers.

Zig Ziglar, the great sales trainer, put it this way, "You get what *you* want by helping other people get what *they* want." Live by it. It works.

Follow the leaders. The Zig Ziglars and the Paul Meyers of the world are on top. They didn't get there by lying, cheating, or stealing. They got there by serving. When you create an organization that "lives to serve," you will succeed—even if your prices *are* higher.

Your advertising communicates who you are, what you stand for, and what your business stands for. Why not communicate your commitment to the customer—and the community—in your advertising? Survey after survey reveals that people prefer to buy from businesses they see as more socially responsible. If your products are healthier, more environmentally friendly, more animal friendly—say it! Make sure this message comes through loud and clear in your advertising.

Let's take it to the next level. How can we stay on top, continue to lead, communicate our commitment to the community—and still drive home a selling message? When I said leaders' advertising needs to "grow a conscience," I meant just that. Get involved in cause-related marketing.

Of course, everyone's favorite radio station is WIFM—*What's in It For Me?* Altruism aside, there's a lot in it for you. Let's look at this strictly from a business point of view. When you become the leader and act like the leader, people of like mind will gravitate to you.

With the number of people that die of cancer and heart disease each year, think how many families are touched by these diseases. That means you are surrounded by people who have lost loved ones to these killer diseases. Promote your involvement in helping to wipe them out, and you'll develop a following—and that's what leaders do.

Take up a cause you can be passionate about. Then:

- Set aside a portion of your advertising dollar for cause-related marketing.
- Devote some of the funds to direct donations.
- Designate some money for sponsorship of cause-related events.
- Earmark your advertising to indicate your support of these causes.
- Use the unique leverage your business provides to rally support for your cause.
- Sponsor a radiothon or telethon.
- Establish a scholarship fund on behalf of an afflicted child.

For example, if you're in the food business, run a food drive. If you're in the clothing business, run a clothing drive. Step out of the box; change hats. Do the unconventional and unexpected—*invite your competitors* to a friendly contest to see who can raise the most money.

Ultimately, your community will see you as a leader who supports their causes. In turn, they will continue to support your business. And your success will have bred true success, not complacency.

TOOLBOX

When your competition's products, presentation, and advertising start to look and sound strangely like yours, you can congratulate yourself; you've become the leader.

❮❮ Time Capsule: "Eat at Louis's"

Perhaps you don't understand why leaders need to develop a conscience, or how that can help your business. Perhaps you don't understand Louis the XIV either. We'll clear this up for you in no time.

To demonstrate, we'll fire up the way-back machine and visit his Palace of Versailles—the ultimate catering establishment. See, right here is a chamber orchestra—knowing Louis, it must be a benefit concert for the homeless.

And that glittering banquet in the Hall of Mirrors? Obviously, he's honoring all the generous titled nobility who have aided the community. And finally, we find Louis himself in a back room, counting piles of gold coins, evidently organizing a lottery for the less fortunate.

He's so modest about this stuff, really; he never publicizes his good works. Going down the road in the fancy coach with the drapes drawn, a cavalry detachment clearing the road in front of him, you'd think he was being haughty instead of just shy.

Think of how many people he feeds in a year. Does the public know about that? Did you see all that wine? Do you have any idea how many people he keeps employed, just by buying all that wine? I'll bet half of the countryside owes him their lives—I mean, livelihoods.

Try to understand this from a marketing perspective. Louis the XIV is really in the *hospitality* business. That's another way of saying he's in the business of providing comfort to his guests. At any cost, true, but that just shows his *dedication*.

Here's what really galls me—think of all the missed marketing opportunities! Louis could be holding croquet matches in those fabulous gardens. He could charge people to sponsor the players, even the mallets—the possibilities are *unlimited!* Your business can have signage in the gardens of the royal palace—talk about targeting a quality demographic group! You could have embossed napkins at the banquet; announcements made during the croquet match; ads in the program; your name on the place cards at the table, etc., and it's all to raise money for a worthy cause—the royal family!

And there are people who think all this is just wretched excess at the public's expense. Obviously, the guy needs a better PR firm. Could you take a lesson from this man, on how to promote *your* leadership? Pass that bottle of Baron Lafitte, please. **»**

The Highlight Zone: "Beware of Anyone Bearing Gifts"

Submitted for your approval, Geoffrey Kraemer, owner of Kraemer's Lighting Emporium. He is taking care of customers when an elderly gentleman enters the shop with a burning question.

"Would you take this lamp, please, sir?" asks the old man. "It's been in my family for years, but I just can't bear to look at it. Whenever I do, I just think of all the family members that have died. I really don't want anything for it, I just want to be free of the memories."

Geoffrey saw that the lamp was valuable and assured the old man it would find a good home.

All day, he kept glancing over at the lamp. He thought of the ancient Greek Diogenes, walking around the city of Athens in broad daylight, with a lighted lamp. When asked why, Diogenes replied, "I am looking for an honest man."

Mr. Kraemer could have sold the lamp and kept the money, honestly. Or he could have taken it home. Instead, he decided to auction it to the highest bidder and donate the proceeds to a nursing home.

When he arrived to present the check, the same old man that brought in the lamp greeted him. Meanwhile, it just happened that the day Mr. Kraemer chose to visit the home, there was an open-house celebration. Family members of the residents were there. And in the weeks that followed, many of those same children miraculously found their way to Kraemer's Lighting Emporium.

Did our Mr. Geoffrey Kraemer enter another dimension with his business? Perhaps—one glowing with promise.

chapter 10

I'm Doing Just Fine . . . I Don't Need to Advertise

"I have so much business, I couldn't handle any more if it walked through my doors."

Wanna bet? Those words may chase away advertising salespeople, but they seldom ring true. Usually you hear it from small businesses that claim to be able to handle their own advertising.

Let's see how well you're really doing. Take this Advertising IQ Test, and see for yourself. When you find out how little you really know about advertising, you may reconsider your position on this matter. That done, you may discover that you can attract a lot more business with effective advertising. Very likely, you will find a way to handle the additional business.

Moreover, when you take a look at the forces continually eroding your business, you'll want to fortify yourself with some well-planned and well-executed advertising.

ADVERTISING IQ TEST

True or False:

1. Curiosity-arousing ads work best.
2. A picture is worth a thousand words.

3. The most important thing in an ad is the headline, followed by the caption under the photo or illustration.
4. People remember what they see better than what they hear.
5. To the consumer, perception is reality.
6. Celebrity spokespeople create better brand identities.
7. Companies that stopped advertising during recessions fared better than their competitors.
8. Price is more important to consumers than anything else.
9. Everyone who reads the newspaper will see your ad.
10. Outdoor advertising has the lowest cost-reach ratio of all major media.

Ready for a few surprises? Pay careful attention to the answers that follow.

Now, the Answers

1. *Curiosity-arousing ads work best.* False. John Caples, former vice president of BBD&O, one of the world's largest ad agencies, distinguished himself as the king of direct-response. In his book, *Tested Advertising Methods*, Caples describes the results of years of tests with thousands of ads. Caples ran direct response mail-order magazine ads, testing different headlines. Time and time again, he discovered that curiosity simply did not pull in orders.

Headlines with a *strong consumer benefit* out-pulled all others, followed by those with newsworthiness. Caples achieved the optimum result by combining a consumer benefit with newsworthiness.

Here's a simple example of a headline that combines a consumer benefit with a newsworthy item: "Recent American Dental Association Tests Prove That Crest Fights Cavities Better than the Nearest Leading Toothpaste."

The benefit? Fights cavities. The news? ADA tests prove. . . .

2. *A picture is worth a thousand words.* False. Jack Trout and Al Ries, advertising partners who have written some iconoclastic books on the subject, conducted detailed research. Notwithstanding the differing learning styles of consumers, they found that, "A word is worth a thousand pictures." People are more verbally oriented.

3. *The most important thing in an ad is the headline, followed by the caption under the photo or illustration.* True. David Ogilvy, the dean of American advertising, discovered that people paging through a publication typically skim headlines, then go to captions. Even if they fail to read the body copy in a print ad, a well-written headline and caption will still get the message across to even the cursory reader.

4. *People remember what they see better than what they hear.* False. Once again, Trout and Ries proved that audio messages have higher recall. Cigarette advertising provides the most dramatic example. Ask anyone over the age of forty to sing cigarette jingles. Even astute businesspeople have difficulty remembering a newspaper ad they read the same day, yet can remember cigarette ads that were banned from the airwaves in 1970!

5. *To the consumer, perception is reality.* True. People see and hear what they *think* an ad said—not necessarily the actual content. During the Christmas season in 1983, we innocently ran a radio commercial for a local camera shop promoting the Kodak disk camera. The ad stated, "Get a Kodak disk camera for 1984." Customers insisted we said $19.84. The camera retailed for about $50.

Similarly, an auto dealer group promoted "Get four Fords for $7,777." They meant to say, "Buy any one of four models at this price." Someone sued, insisting he should get all four cars for $7,777. Oops—he won!

Recently, en route to an appointment, I hurriedly pulled up to a highway tollbooth. Concerned for time, I asked the Asian-American toll taker, "How far to exit 98?" He replied, "Not far." My initial frustration over not knowing any more than I did before soon subsided, as I realized that to get the answer I wanted I should have phrased the question, "How many miles?" or "How many minutes?" However, in his cultural frame of reference, he perceived that he had answered the question perfectly. He had answered the question correctly—I had asked the wrong question.

Not only is perception reality, but perceptions are largely culturally determined—male and female, ethnic subcultures, even life stage can influence and color perceptual differences.

6. *Celebrity spokespeople create better brand identities.* False. Ogilvy insists that consumers remember the spokesperson and not the brand that is being advertised. By and large, he's right. Consider the plethora of actors touting discount long distance phone services. Do you remember which one represents which service?

The only exception involves a spokesperson with a natural tie-in, such as Michael Jordan for Nike sneakers. Large companies still pay out absurdly high endorsement fees to celebrities, in spite of the public's inability to relate them to the product being advertised. Don't fall into that trap.

That said, I hasten to point out the difference between celebrity brand spokespeople and personality endorsements. Within the context of a live radio broadcast, for example, if the show host reads a commercial and personally endorses the quality or value of the product, it can substantially *increase* response. That audience identifies with the host, and believes what he or she says. The affinity between them creates a favorable selling environment for the product. This creates audience "buy-in." Very simply, the right product endorsed by the right host, promoted to the right audience spells SUCCESS.

I'll give just a few brief examples. Paul Harvey is the single most listened-to radio personality in America—even though his program only airs for segments of five to fifteen minutes. His credibility with his audience is supreme. If Paul Harvey says buy it, they will. He has built brands like Monsanto Floor Covering, Wahl Shaver-Trimmers, the Bose Wave Radio, and a host of others.

At the opposite end of the cultural spectrum from Paul Harvey is Howard Stern, who commands the same fanatical loyalty from a different age group. Stern built the Snapple beverage brand—no doubt about it!

Small businesses across the United States have discovered the value of personality endorsements. They do not cost anywhere near what big-time celebrity spokespeople cost, and they probably work even better. We've used them successfully for travel agencies and cruise lines. When a popular local radio personality announces that he or she plans to take a cruise and invites his or her audience to come along, they sign up. We recently ran one of these promotions for an Alaska trip. Eighty-eight people signed up, at a cost of about $3,200 each (including airfare). That's a $280,000 return on an advertising investment of $20,000.

Our client, Reviva Labs, manufactures a line of anti-aging skin care products for women. The company identified markets where they wanted to support stores and salons carrying the product. We identified strong female air personalities who were themselves over the age of forty, with radio audiences of women age forty and over. We then sent product samples ahead, inviting them to test the formula. Once they were satisfied the product worked, they agreed to endorse it, and we began to air the commercials. The impact of the friend you trust for daily advice telling you to buy the product is incalculable.

Radio personalities, local television talk show hosts, newspaper and magazine columnists—anyone with a high degree of well-established credibility in a field related to yours can help you achieve this. Central Holidays, a tour operator, hired a professional photographer to escort an exotic photo safari, advertising the trip in a travel magazine. WCCO-AM Radio in Minneapolis has hosted trips for thirty-five years, involving everyone from cooking show hosts to meteorologists.

7. *Companies that stopped advertising during recessions fared better than their competitors.* False. Studies show that companies that continued to advertise during recessions kept (and sometimes gained) market share, while those that stopped advertising irretrievably lost market share.

8. *Price is more important to consumers than anything else.* False. U.S. Department of Commerce studies as far back as the 1970s indicate that price ranks fifth in importance when consumers decide where to shop. Convenience rules in today's economy. Witness the rise of an entire industry based on convenience: convenience grocery stores. In those stores people pay much more for items readily available in supermarkets and drugstores, to save precious time.

9. *Everyone who reads the newspaper will see your ad.* False. Readership studies by Roper Starch Worldwide, a market research firm, prove that many ads are not even noticed, let alone read. We achieved better results with auto dealer ads that were less than full page if they were "page dominant." Many people

flipped past the full page-ads, yet stopped to glance at an ad on a page with some editorial content.

Circulation-penetration reports by the Radio Advertising Bureau indicate that a sizable ad that runs five times in a major daily newspaper might only be recalled by 40 percent or fewer of the publication's readers.

10. *Outdoor advertising has the lowest cost-reach ratio of all major media.* True. However, each medium has its place in your mix. Each accomplishes a specific purpose. Keep in mind that an effective billboard has nine words or less. You may need print, broadcast, or direct mail to tell your whole story. If your product's purchasing cycle is long and infrequent, for example, radio's recall may prove valuable.

TOOLBOX

Reinforce your print ads with radio—people remember what they hear much longer than what they read.

Be honest. So, what's your Advertising IQ? Hopefully, you learned something new from the exercise. But don't stop there. Review the recommended reading list in the Appendix of this book. Otherwise, you're at least in danger of reinventing the wheel.

More importantly, hopefully you now see that there is always more that your advertising can do, meaning that there is always more business to get.

And even if you don't see that, surely you at least don't want to lose what business you already have. The U.S. Department of Commerce tells us the average business loses 20 percent of its customer base every year through normal attrition. Add to that any specific market conditions that might affect your business (such as plant closings or relocations that erode your customer base; urban decay; or large, well-financed competitors moving into your trading area), and it's clear that we all need to keep advertising just to stay even.

But you say that you want to go beyond survival? You say that you want to grow? Well, that's what this book is for, to keep the price of advertising down and the results up.

PROFESSIONALS NEED ANSWERS

Now, when it comes to Advertising IQ, we have to start all over again if you are in one of the licensed professions. Certain ads may or may not work—but that is not the first consideration. First, before embarking on an ad campaign for your professional practice, you must check with your regulatory agencies.

Every state has different rules. For example, can you promise results? Do you have to disclaim anything? Are you allowed to include a dramatization? Can you post prices? Often, regulatory authorities spot-check ads that come to their attention. Sometimes, they issue fines—without even giving a warning.

There was a time when many professions were completely barred from advertising. Doctors, dentists, lawyers, and others could not legally use most advertising media. Times change. Needs change. Eventually, laws change. With increased competition, economic pressures forced these groups to promote their practices. In many states, it is now legal, but the advertising for these groups is highly regulated.

But that does not mean it is well regulated. We are still in the early stages of legalized professional advertising, and the authorities are still finding their way. I can remember calling my state board of medical examiners to inquire if the promotion we had in mind was, in fact, legal. No one knew.

Of course, in most states, you can get a highly specific set of regulations governing car dealer advertising practices for the asking. But ask for the same thing for opticians or dentists, and you get this mantra: "Tell us what you have in mind, and we'll tell you if it's permitted."

Aside from regulatory hassles, for a long time, professionals have been their own worst enemy when it came to advertising. True, they should want to maintain dignity and decorum. However, without having "Crazy Ralph's Discount Eye Surgery in an Hour," you can still allow professionals to promote their practices and compete as businesspeople—which is, in fact, what they are.

But when things go wrong, another issue crops up: Who is responsible for the correctness and compliance of your ads? You, your ad agency, or your attorney?

In truth, you *all* are. Ultimately, it's your ad, it's your business, and it's *your* responsibility to see that your counselors review it. I recently met with a dentist who pointed to a brochure he gives his patients. It states that he trains other dentists in a procedure. He now has to document that to his state authority—after getting fined! Beware of professional jealousy. More than likely, a rival dentist turned him in for this minor "infraction."

Don't forget your professional associations. In many cases, they have their own self-regulatory bodies. Once you have satisfied your state laws, you may still have to submit your intended ad campaign to your professional association for further review. The intent is to gain positive awareness—remember brand preference? But in the meantime you don't need to give a jealous competitor any fuel for his or her fire by failing to comply with both legal and professional regulators.

If all this compliance seems onerous, it is. However, it's worth it to build and to keep a good name. You can't grow a practice on word-of-mouth alone anymore. Consider getting both legal and advertising counsel with direct experience in your profession. Have they ever advertised for or defended another doctor, dentist, etc.? If so, were there any violations while they handled the account? (That should be a matter of public record!)

Do It with Dignity

Let's examine some of the ways a professional practice can advertise without appearing crass. Ironically, attorneys who advertise are probably the worst offenders when it comes to crassness. We typically think of them as "ambulance chasers," but it doesn't have to be done that way. Following, you'll find some ways that lawyers, doctors, and other professionals can advertise and promote their practices without appearing undignified. Any business, especially a service business, can make use of these same techniques.

Hold an Open House

Invite only those people who are "centers of influence." These are community leaders, each with influence over a circle of people. They include the local chamber of commerce officers; leaders of civic clubs like Rotary, Kiwanis, Lions, etc.; local government officials; and respected academicians (college or university deans, trustees, etc.).

This gives you a firsthand, belly-to-belly opportunity to showcase your practice, to demonstrate your sincerity, and to persuade community leaders of your capabilities—who will, in turn, refer the people in their circle to you.

Suggestion: Have a contact person in your office make a telephone call ahead, mail the invitations, and follow up by telephone. Also, send a thank-you note to each person invited, whether they attended or not.

Conduct Offsite Seminars

You're the expert in your field. In this complicated world, everyone craves knowledge. Just watch what happens when you attend a party. Invariably, someone discovers your profession, and the questions start flowing—from traffic violations to new drug therapies.

Offer your knowledge and skills to the local civic and business groups you invited to your open house. These groups often need and want expert speakers. Fashion your topic carefully; tailor it to the makeup of the group. For example, if you're an attorney speaking to the local unit of the National Association of Women Business Owners (NAWBO), talk to them about estate planning for women.

By appearing at these events, you're in a nonthreatening, nonselling environment. You're the expert. If you're a stimulating speaker, people will gravitate to you after the event. That's your chance to pick up new clients.

Hopefully, the group will promote your appearance. But don't depend on it. Ask them if you can promote it yourself. Advertising your appearance at a function as a guest speaker is highly dignified. In the best-case scenario, members of the group will invite you to speak before other groups they belong to.

Become "The Source"

Create an ad campaign that is educational and informative. Run a series of ads in the medium of your choice—newspaper, magazine, radio, or cable TV. Compose each ad as if it were an article or an excerpt from a speech. Alternately, they can mimic a "how-to" or advice column. Even if you are required to place the word "Advertisement" on the ads, if they look like and read or sound like editorial matter, people will pay attention to them—and believe them more readily.

This approach is a "soft sell" method of keeping your name in front of the public, and positioning you as the expert, by offering knowledge.

I once ran a series of radio ads like this for a holistic dentist. He explained how he would take a history on a new patient and discover nutritional problems that were—pardon the pun—the root cause of the decline in their dental health. We recorded these ads in an interview style, with questions and answers. At the end, we simply tagged on, "For an appointment or consultation, call Doctor Steiner at. . . . "

Opportunistic Ads

Suppose a well-loved doctor in your community is about to retire. What will happen to his patients? You can't buy out his or her practice;

you found out too late. You can, however, run ads saluting his or her fine contribution, and inviting the patients to come to you for a similar quality of care. It helps if you can get the retiring physician's blessing on this one.

As delicate as the subject is, you can employ the same strategy in the event of someone's death. After all, those clients or patients have to go somewhere—so they might as well come to you. Once again, don't wait for a miracle. Make it (the ads, not the death) happen.

Set Up a Web Site

Just remember to create an ad campaign offline, to promote the site. This could be as simple as sending postcards to the editors of various special-interest or occupational trade association newsletters, directing them to the site.

While you're online, consider creating a newsgroup or a blog (Web log) on the Internet, or joining an existing newsgroup in your field. Begin a dialogue on a hot issue. For example, if you're an accountant, explain a new tax law change, point out how it helps or hurts the public, and invite responses. You will garner attention, showcase your expertise—and possibly attract new clients.

TOOLBOX

Professionals need to advertise—but with great care. Don't offend the regulators, your colleagues, or the public.

Expect a Flood

But regardless of whether you are in a professional or commercial field, no matter how much business you have today, at any time, it can go away. All it takes is one military base to close, and a town's customer base—and revenue base—floats downstream. Don't count on the government to come in and rebuild your economy.

Nor does it have to be a military base. The entire town of Manville, New Jersey, was severely impacted by the closing of the Johns-Manville asbestos factory. There have been many Manvilles across the country. What would you do, if you had one in your town?

Well, the first thing you might do is to become part of the solution. If your community does experience either a natural disaster or a commercial disaster, join the relief effort. You'll help out; you'll feel good—and you'll probably get some publicity. Better yet, devote a portion of your advertising to promoting how others can help those affected. Advertise your location as an information center, drop-off center, counseling center, etc.

In the meantime, part of the readiness means that you will continue to market, advertise, and promote your business, so as to be prepared when the Great Flood sweeps your customers away. Because the fact that there is no flood in progress, nor any sign of rain, does not mean it can't happen tomorrow.

Will you be ready? If you own and operate the kind of "bootstrap" start-up that we do, you probably will. You know what it takes to succeed. You know that "Let the good times roll" may be a great adage for living your life with zest, but it won't cut it when it comes to entrepreneurship.

While the guys across town are playing golf and buying boats, we're burning the midnight oil, doing one and a half day's work in each day. They're thinking they're sitting pretty, living on the money they raised. We're living day-to-day, knowing tomorrow is just as uncertain as today.

When it's your money, every ad has to work. Every nickel counts. Everything is measured in ROI (Return On Investment). Tomorrow, if the stock market tanks and their investors get nervous, we keep moving—without the big overhead.

I grew up as a child of Depression-era parents. They imparted the "save it for a rainy day" mentality to me. Well, I've been high and dry at some times and I've been soaked at others. Thanks to my upbringing,

I've always had an "umbrella" of sorts. What will the other guys do when the flood comes? I don't know, but I'll be ready.

TOOLBOX

Even if your business is at its best today, promote as if you had to start over tomorrow, and you'll stay ahead.

But the Water Always Recedes

When you realize how uncertain your business future really is, you'll appreciate the need to keep advertising—no matter how busy or successful you were in the past, or how busy or successful you are today. The fact is that every business stands to lose trade, through no fault of its own. Meanwhile, with the arrival of one or more well-financed new competitors cutting into your slice of the pie, there goes the whipped cream!

You must keep the pipeline full of new business. Unless there is a huge influx of new people coming into your market, you have to expect to lose business—and you have to have a plan ready to replace that lost business.

If you're thinking, "You're just saying that because you're an ad man yourself," then don't take my word for it—ask your old friend, Mr. History. Just look at the last downturn. As we mentioned in the Advertising IQ Test, studies prove that businesses which kept advertising in bad times kept their market share, or increased it.

Even the term "good times" is relative. Good for whom? If you're flush now, but you're working with OPM (Other People's Money), see how long that lasts when the economy slows down.

Just like a surfer, if you plan to ride the wave, you have to stay ahead of the wave. Reinvesting profits in advertising and promotion just ensures that people will continue to patronize you.

A word to my friends and colleagues in the professions: If you haven't figured it out by now, today's business climate affects you like never before. With the glut of law school graduates, with the consolidation of hospital systems, with the advent of managed health care, with the amount of do-it-yourself, off-the-shelf accounting software, you need to learn how to promote yourselves and compete as businesses—not just as practitioners. Do it with style, do it with class, do it with dignity, but *do it every day.*

❮❮ Time Capsule: "Eat at Ben's"

Dining is universal. They even did it in Philadelphia in the time of Ben Franklin. So let's do lunch at his place.

I noticed we had to pass through the print shop to get seated in the restaurant. On the plus side, they have to see one business in order to patronize the other. It may get a little noisy, but you can never have too much business.

Now, here's what I like best about the place. Ben's analyzed his market, and each day he has a different menu insert for a separate professional group. Monday is lawyer's day; Tuesday is doctor's day; Wednesday is merchant's day, etc.

Look at this. "Guaranteed service to all who can pay." I get it—if you promise prompt seating and you serve them quickly, you turn the tables over faster and you don't turn anyone away.

Now, what keeps that professional crowd coming back, Ben? Right—they put their cards on that board by the window. And each day one person gets picked at random to make a speech. Best of all, Ben buys him lunch that day. And on the back of the menu insert, there's a newsletter that recaps yesterday's speech.

Now, we really must be going. Of course, we'd love to hear your speech on how to decrease the rat population in Philadelphia, Dr. Moriarity, but we do have some problems to solve ourselves.

The way I see it, Mr. Franklin's quite a marketer. Think about it. He's got this captive crowd coming in for printing, smelling the aroma of the food. Meanwhile, he's got the restaurant patrons reading a wall full of calling cards printed in his shop, a menu printed in his shop, a newsletter printed in his shop. Best of all, he's provided this forum of exchange for businesses and professional practices. Think how much they all patronize one another. It's like a daily expo, where you can get right up close and personal. **》**

The Highlight Zone: "Yesterday's News Is Tomorrow's Tragedy"

The time: the present. The place: a large city in the American Midwest. The occasion: a gathering of businesspeople, celebrating their success. As we listen in on the conversation, we hear each man and woman talk about how well he or she did last year.

Then, one person decides to turn up the television set, right at the beginning of an urgent bulletin. A flood has wiped out two neighboring towns. Several thousand homes and businesses have been destroyed.

That means each of the business owners in the room has suddenly lost a large percentage of last year's customers. How many of them can or will come back after rebuilding? How long will that take?

And they suddenly realize that complacency has no place in the modern business world. No matter how much business you have, there is no guarantee it will be there next year, next month, next week—or tomorrow.

What will you do to keep the momentum going and to protect you against whatever disasters lie ahead? Because there are no laurels to rest on, especially not in the Highlight Zone.

part 2

MORE WAYS TO SCREW UP AN AD CAMPAIGN

Now that you know the basics of what works and what doesn't, let's take a more in-depth look at how to really make your advertising rock!

chapter 11

Does Your Advertising Measure Up . . . or Does Your Measurement Measure Up?

Perhaps the greatest concern of every businessperson revolves around the issue of measurement. How do I track my advertising results? As department store owner John Wanamaker said, "Fifty percent of my advertising doesn't work. The only problem is, I don't know which 50 percent."

Alas, little has changed—there is still no *single* effective yardstick with which to measure your advertising results. However, taken together, several methods will give you a picture. The main ones are listed below—*use as many as apply* in any situation.

1. Make a specific offer (SO) in one advertising medium alone. Make sure that it does *not* appear in your other ads.
2. Likewise, use a dedicated phone number (DPN) in one advertising medium. See that it does *not* appear in your other ads.
3. Look at ZIP codes (ZC) of the customers who responded to a particular campaign. If you traditionally pull from a limited geography and now see people responding from a wider area, it may indicate results from a new campaign in a new advertising medium.

4. Look at the demographics (DEM) of the customers who responded to a campaign. If, for example, you usually draw older men and now you see younger people and more women, it may indicate that new medium is working for you.

5. Be careful about asking customers to tell you how they heard about you. Unless the campaign was extraordinarily focused, you will often be disappointed or confused by the results. Consumers seldom can accurately identify which medium brought them in. Take the phenomenon of "last reference"—if you ask a customer how they found you, they may say, "The Yellow Pages." In reality, all your other advertising led them to pick your ad out of the Yellow Pages. They simply told you the *last* place they saw you prior to responding.

6. Cross-check. Ask people what media they usually read, watch, or listen to. Even though they did not volunteer seeing or hearing your ad, or remember when prompted, if they do read, watch, or listen to the media you are using, chances are it helped bring them to you.

Accordingly, here is your "advertising yardstick." Turn it into a checklist when you evaluate post-campaign results. Use every inch of it, and use it wisely.

- ☐ SO (Special Offer)
- ☐ UR (Unaided Recall—refers to customers volunteering where they heard about you, without any suggestions from you.)
- ☐ AR (Aided Recall—refers to customers selecting ways they heard about you from a list of choices you provide.)
- ☐ ZC (ZIP Code)
- ☐ DPN (Dedicated Phone Number)
- ☐ DEM (Demographic—age, race, sex)

"NOBODY MENTIONED SEEING MY AD"

Improper measurement and the resulting misattribution of advertising results ranks high on the list of the most abused practice in small-business advertising—next to hiring brothers-in-law and spouses as marketing directors. You can see it in action in the following scenario.

Mr. Elliott Thwackhammer of the ACME Insurance Company has decided to rush to market with the company's new variable annuity product. Mr. Thwackhammer has no market research to help him determine who will buy this product. He naturally assumes people like himself are the ideal candidates. Accordingly:

- He runs an ad in his Sunday newspaper's sports section.
- He sponsors some local college football broadcasts.
- He mails a letter to all homes within ten miles of his office.

What happens next?

Monday morning arrives. At the ACME Insurance Company, the only busy office machine is the coffee machine. But phones are ringing, calls are coming to Mr. Thwackhammer's desk—the boss wants a full report of the results of this "advertising nonsense" by the end of the day.

Five o'clock rolls around. Mr. Thwackhammer has written five policies that day. All of them are from new clients, but only three bought the new annuity product. Two more calls come in after five o'clock from coworkers of the new customers. One bought; the other scheduled an appointment.

But that darned advertising report still hangs over his head. It looks like the boss isn't leaving, so Mr. Thwackhammer will have to write it and miss the cocktail hour at the country club.

Elliott hands in the report. The boss reviews it. And grumbles.

"So, no results at all from this 'advertising thing' you did? How did you determine that?"

Elliott looks at the boss, a bit downtrodden. "Well, none of the callers mentioned seeing or hearing any of the ads. When I asked, only one remembered getting my letter at home. I guess we won't do that again."

Is this how you're evaluating your advertising? If so, take another look at the scenario. Here are the *right* questions to ask, to properly evaluate the results of Mr. Thwackhammer's ad campaign.

- How many policies does he normally write in a day? Was there an uptick in volume that might have come from the advertising?
- What programs in what media do these new customers usually read, watch, listen to? If you ask this as a cross-check, you may find that they *did* actually see or hear your ads, even though they didn't remember them.
- Since he advertised a new product, chances are minimal that anyone *not* exposed to the advertising would know to call him for it.
- Did these new customers come from parts of town not previously well represented in the company's customer base?
- Could it be that some of the day's callers were responding to the advertising but ended up being sold other products that fit their needs better?

When you examine all of the above items, it looks like ACME's advertising did, in fact, work.

Meanwhile, keep in mind that certain audiences are more *vocal* than others. They make a point of demonstrating loyalty to their favorite media outlet and its sponsor. For example, country and western music fans, fans of certain politically charged talk radio shows, and cutting-edge rock fans are more inclined to let you know they patronized you because you sponsor their favorite program. Christian radio also generates advertiser loyalty—but the fans are quieter. As for the bulk of the world, don't wait for them to volunteer where they saw or heard your ads; you'll only disappoint yourself. Even the most intelligent people often can't remember.

So the question is not how your advertising measures up. The real question is, how does the *measurement* of your advertising measure up?

If you re-evaluate your current and previous ad campaigns using our yardstick above, you may find a few surprises. The medium you thought didn't work may actually have worked. Furthermore, if you apply this type of measurement to your *next* campaign, you may change your mind about some of your media choices.

TOOLBOX

Focus on results—don't obsess over which advertising medium worked best. Fully examine all the hidden factors that might have contributed to your sales volume during the campaign. Dig deeper before you decide what worked and what didn't.

WHEN? WHEN? WHEN TO ADVERTISE?

Answer: all the time.

You say you can't afford to do that? Then advertise the most at the times when you stand to *get* the most business. "Pulsing" may prove your most successful strategy.

Pulsing involves keeping a constant, but light advertising schedule, then adding to it during peak sales periods. During those times, you run larger ads or more frequent commercials.

Meanwhile, by changing from an institutional (a generic name-location ad) to a sale/event message (an ad focusing on a special sale or promotion), combined with the increased presence, should kick up your response level. At the same time, the ad doesn't have to "work as hard" because the audience already knows who you are.

Remember the story in an earlier chapter of the hardware store that ran extra commercials during the cold winter weather, promoting the truckload sale of kerosene heaters? That was a form of pulsing.

Meanwhile, there are many advertising people who will tell you that you should be spending the lion's share of your ad budget when business is slowest. But my experience goes totally against this, and it certainly does not fit with the concept of pulsing. With pulsing, you can make your sales peaks higher, and that will help get you through the valleys. There is no reason to try to climb uphill.

For instance, 60 percent of all retail jewelry purchases occur during the Christmas-Chanukah holiday season. For that reason, I budgeted 80 percent of my jewelry client's dollars during this period. The remaining 20 percent went for Mother's Day, their second biggest sales volume period.

COPY DO'S AND DON'TS

Of course, let's not forget that your advertising has to say something. The written part of an ad is called "the copy" (regardless of whether you are copying anything), and there is bad copy writing and good copy writing. Ad campaigns have been killed by the former and rescued by the latter. Follow the tips below and you should not kill—or even wound—any campaigns.

Avoid ad exhaustion—concentrate on your unique selling proposition. When an advertiser tries to make an ad work too hard, it drops dead from exhaustion. Don't try to list your entire inventory in one ad. Instead, ask yourself what really differentiates you from the competition.

Beware the cliché trap. "We give personalized service." Everyone says that. It has lost its power in an ad. Instead, tell people how you do what you do better. Do you spend more time with customers, educating them? Do you offer pickup or delivery?

Extended hours? Don't take for granted that the competition does exactly what you do.

Don't bury the benefits. Too many advertisers do just that. In your ads, tell them right up front. Mark Twain's advice to writers bears mentioning: "Don't say 'The old lady screamed'; bring her on and let her scream."

Give people tangible benefits, identifiable savings, and a good value perception. Saying "10 percent off" is meaningless in a world where people are jaded with "50 percent off" and "buy one, get one" offers. But if you're selling high-end furniture, that 10 percent savings may represent several hundred dollars. Tell them *that*, and they'll come.

Inject some sense of urgency and a call to action. Tell them why they should respond now, and make sure your ad "asks for the order." Without a believable reason for customers to buy now, they will wait—possibly forever. Or they might respond to someone else's ad before your next (better written) ad appears.

Wake them up! One of my retail clients ran a home decorating center. After adding carpet and window treatments to his paint and wallpaper store, we found the public still didn't know he had expanded his offerings. We ran a small newspaper ad with a photo of him standing on his head on one of his carpets, bearing the headline, "Think How Good It Feels to *Walk* On." The reaction was overwhelming.

Use testimonials. Feature your customers in your ads. They're your best spokespeople. Real people from your prospects' own community are highly credible. Use this approach if you're new in business, or if you're in an industry that people don't have a high regard for. Real, believable, local testimonials help to *create trust*. Remember the story of the pain relief product with the doctor reading the letters customers sent in to the company?

Appeal to basic instincts. Everyone wants to make money, save money, look better, feel smarter, and achieve status and prestige. Speak to these needs.

Stay focused on what you're really selling. Hotels don't sell rooms, they offer *comfort.* Remember the swimming pool store? We wrote his commercials around the theme of "the vacation that lasts a lifetime."

Tickle the imagination. Your prospective customers should be able to project themselves into the ad. Help them visualize themselves enjoying the benefits they will derive from your product or service. It might read something like this: "You're lying in the hammock with the warm sun dancing across your eyelids, the gentle breeze caressing your hair, oblivious to the calendar back home on your doorstep, as the rain soaks the page labeled 'December.'"

Get a little outrageous. Cut through the clutter. Remember the exercise where we asked you to create a deadly ad, instead of a dead one?

Pull some magic out of your bag of tricks. What do I mean? Some devices never get tired. In the right hands, they can wow an audience. For example, *hyperbole* is a form of poetic exaggeration. Comedian Stan Frieberg wrote the radio ad where they filled the imaginary lake with chocolate, to make giant chocolate bars. Your prospects' imaginations are the most powerful tools you have to work with. (You can do that cheaply on the radio.) This is a great way to differentiate your product, service, or establishment—especially if it is a look-alike or sound-alike, similar to many others.

Personification is another great one. You give human qualities to some inanimate object. For example, if you sell auto parts, your car can talk—or cry—or laugh at what you're "feeding it." Again, these work especially well on radio, because the mind can imagine anything you conjure up, without expensive production. (In the next chapter, I'll give you some actual examples of big impact, highly memorable ads I created for some very small businesses.)

Appeal to all of the senses. We produced a series of cable television commercials for a chain of plumbing supply stores. Without increasing the budget, we wanted to inject a human element. People respond better to products shown in use than to cold, empty rooms. We took the manufacturer's supplied footage of bathroom fixtures and ran background sound effects of children at play. They weren't on camera; we didn't have to pay actors and shoot new footage, but to the viewer, *they were there.*

In advertising, the three most important elements are repetition, repetition, and repetition. Repeat your company name; repeat your offer; repeat your benefits—again, and again, and again. Should I repeat that? Educators and trainers generally agree that it takes six repetitions of an idea for people to learn new information, or to change habits. You not only need to repeat your ads to succeed, you need to repeat your name *within* each ad. For example, I usually try to put my client's name *four to six times* in one sixty-second radio ad.

Go for the "big idea." Find a theme you can hang a whole campaign on. We created a radio campaign for a small chain of record stores that resulted in people coming in and chanting the store name "Sound-A-Rama" the way our character in the ad did. The advertiser wouldn't let go of it. We just kept creating more variations on the same theme. It never got tired. Then there was our "History of Wheels" auto dealer campaign that we took from the Stone Age to Hannibal crossing the Alps, stopping in ancient Egypt, Greece, and Rome along the way.

Capitalize on archetypes and expectations, not stereotypes. People naturally associate certain products with certain characters, treatments, and presentations. Years ago, a Chevrolet dealer group ran a very successful singing commercial about "baseball, apple pie, and Chevrolet."

Have fun with it. They will, too, and they'll appreciate you for it.

In this chapter, we told you how to evaluate your advertising, how to determine when to advertise, and how to get your prospects' attention. Combine that with our earlier advice on where to advertise and what to do after the advertising appears, and you should be ready to rock and roll—or jazz it up. Did you ever notice that nobody ever says "let's classical it up"?

TOOLBOX

All the advertising dollars in the world are only as good as the ads you create. Get it noticed; get it remembered; make them want more.

◀◀ Time Capsule: "Eat at Nappi's"

Next in our examination of the lessons offered by restaurants through the ages, we'll have dinner at Napoleon's Palace. The place poses some real promotional challenges. But there's one thing about military rulers—they always measure their effectiveness.

Pay special attention to a few promotional devices that just are "oh, so Nappi." Did you notice the trumpeters atop the palace walls? And just look at the way they shoot off the cannons as we arrive. I'll bet everyone in town knows we're visiting. Now, see how General Nappi tracks his advertising at tonight's big bash.

Marie what's-her-name is checking the guest list for new patrons; the archbishop is verifying their church membership and titles of nobility; the captain is checking their tax records. See the foppish looking guy in the white wig? He's in charge of maintaining the database—er, guest list.

Let's see what we've got, so far: a primitive way to check geographic response; an early version of a mail merge program; probably the first demographics check ever. Overall, I'd say Nappi has a pretty good handle on where his responses are coming from.

He could work on the incentives and attract more first-time patrons. Then there's that bad press about dungeons and stuff. Plus, he really needs to address those charges of elitism.

And just think how many more people he could bring in if he had *several* parties going on, back-to-back. If he did the twenty-one gun salute thing out front, with a military ball in the great hall, a maritime theme in the banquet hall for the merchants, and even a beggar's banquet out in the back, he could really bump up his numbers at the gate. Best of all, he'd have *no problem* tracking who came in from which ad! I wonder why *he* never thought of that? **»**

The Highlight Zone: "Soft 'Petal' It"

Submitted for your approval, a start-up business full of energy, enthusiasm, and talent—Jane Foster's Flower Shop. Jane has entrusted the child of her imagination to her younger sister Tammi, herself a budding artist and floral designer. While Jane works with suppliers and fulfills orders, Tammi handles the customers and creates an ad campaign to attract new business.

You've entered another dimension; one where the unknown dominates. Welcome to the Highlight Zone.

Unfortunately for the Fosters, the competing florist knows everyone in town—as well as what they like and how they like it. Worst of all, the other florist has been telling its story a lot longer.

No matter. Jane and Tammi have everything to gain. They'll try anything. This very morning, they sent an arrangement to the morning show host on the local radio station. All morning long, he keeps praising the gesture, and describing how the fragrance wafts through the studio.

When he reads the Fosters' ad, people believe it, and begin calling in orders. Some even drive past the other florist to get there.

Later that day, the evening newspaper carries an ad from Foster's Flowers, introducing their "recycling program." "Bring in your wilted flowers and get a trade-in allowance toward new ones," the ad says.

And so the Foster sisters have made their mark as artists, businesswomen, and good citizens.

That evening, the news cameras follow their senator as he attends his daughter's wedding. Two well-dressed young ladies carry in a large congratulatory wreath in an open box labeled "Foster's Flowers."

Sometimes, actions speak louder than words. Other times, the *right* words carry far and wide. Do you need to turn up the volume on your business?

chapter 12

The Harvest: Ads That Rang Phones, Doorbells, and Cash Registers

By now, you have a pretty good idea of what it takes to plan, create, and execute a successful ad campaign. Still, it might help you to see some actual examples of how small businesses attacked their marketing problems. In the examples that follow, you will see the creative components from real ad campaigns that actually ran, created for a wide variety of businesses in vastly different industries.

Although each business's treatment varies, there are common elements among them. Each and every ad differentiates the advertiser from its competitors; each ad plays up the unique benefits of the advertiser; each ad has some built-in device to jog the reader or listener's memory.

There are captions and comments following each ad, describing the techniques used and the results created. See if you and your advertising counsel can adapt some of these same devices to your campaigns.

RADIO

Spot Number 1
Advertiser: Just Dinettes
Length: 60 seconds

Instructions: Opens with first few bars of *Godfather* theme music. Quickly fade and begin dialogue. Dialing sounds, followed by ringing right after the music. Store owner answers the phone, and his voice is casual, friendly, natural.

Godfather: Is this "Just Dinettes"?

Store Owner: This is "Just Dinettes." What can I do for you?

Godfather: Do you sell patio furniture? I'm having a family party.

Store Owner: No, we sell just dinettes.

Godfather: Do you know where I could get a marble table, about fifty feet long? Ya got one in stock?

Store Owner: Sorry, we sell just dinettes.

Godfather: I think I better come down. I wanna take a look at what ya got. I gotta funny feelin' somebody's listenin' in. Tell me how to get there?

Store Owner: We're in Fairless Hills, on Route One. Look for "Just Dinettes" in the northbound lane, by Empress Travel. Anything else I can do for you?

Godfather: Yeah. Play that music again.

Announcer: *(over theme)* "Just Dinettes" pleases even the tough customer. Stop and see their excellent selection.

Spot Number 2

Advertiser: Just Dinettes

Length: 60 seconds

Instructions: Open with first few bars of *Godfather* theme music. Sound effects as indicated. Repeat theme under tag. (Caller's perspective. Phone dialing sound effects; phone rings, and is answered.)

Owner: Hello, Just Dinettes—

Godfather: Just Dinettes? I bought a table from you last week. When's it coming?

Store Owner: Oh, hello Mister "C." Your dinette set should be delivered today. You'll be home, won't you?

Godfather: Oh yeah. I'll be home. No funny stuff, okay?

Store Owner: Funny stuff?

Godfather: What's gonna be in the box?

Store Owner: Just Dinettes.

Godfather: No bombs, no stolen antiques, no smuggled dope?

Store Owner: Just Dinettes.

Godfather: Ya got nice sets there, really nice dinettes. Anyone tell ya that?

Store Owner: All the time. What else did you like about "Just Dinettes"?

Godfather: The prices, the prices. Nice quality. My houseguests were impressed. The whole *family* enjoyed dinner. How much do I owe your driver for the second set?

Store Owner: Nothing, Mister "C." Just Dinettes always delivers free.

Announcer: Just Dinettes, Route One Fairless Hills, opposite Basco. Just Dinettes brings the *family* together.

Analysis: This campaign proved extremely successful. Although it aired on only one small station with a limited audience, it performed for several reasons:

- The continuing word play on the store name "Just Dinettes"
- The repetition of the store name
- The humorous caricature of a familiar, highly recognizable character.

Spot Number 3
Advertiser: The Color Chart/Glidden Paints
Length: 60 seconds

Instructions: Open with UFO sounds; fade same during dialogue. Wife is animated; husband is asleep and unresponsive.

Martha: Harry, look out the window! No, it can't be!

Harry: Whazzat? Huh? Yeah.

Martha: A flying saucer—look—it's skywriting! In *color!*

Harry: What's it say?

Martha: (*reading; broken and choppy delivery*) It says, "Glidden paints are out of this world. Colors that let you create your space. Buy now at the Color Chart."

Harry: Color Chart . . . Color Chart?

Martha: Harry, it's landing! Harry, *do* something.

Harry: (*snores loudly*)

Martha: They're here! They've landed!

Martian: The Color Chart has sent me to invite you to its grand opening. A cosmic event you must not miss. Glidden paints— because you demand the best. Color Chart is the leader for Glidden paints in the Trenton galaxy. Olden Avenue is their launching pad. Please do me one favor.

Martha: Wh-what's that? (*still frightened*)

Martian: Take me to your painter.

Martha: (*over UFO sounds, off-mike.*) HAAAAARRRYYYY!!!

Analysis: With skilled production talent, this commercial grabs listener attention immediately and holds it throughout. It proves how *visual* radio can be. Our imaginations hold the very best pictures.

Spot Number 4

Advertiser: Computerland/Cherry Hill

Length: 60 sec.

Instructions: Wizard of Oz *parody. Stress store name repetitions and fantasy aspect. The Tinman should have metallic-sounding voice with slight echo. "Over the Rainbow" theme music under opening and closing lines.*

Dorothy: This doesn't look *at all* like Camden. I wonder where we are, Toto. *(Dog yips twice.)*

Tinman: You're in Computerland, in a place called Cherry Hill.

Dorothy: Computerland? I only remember the storm of information. I just couldn't keep up with the work—then I woke up here. Oh, will I ever get back home? *(sobs)*

Tinman: Don't cry little girl. In Computerland, there are wonderful machines that can solve so many problems. Why, in Computlerland you can buy an Apple personal computer for your very own!

Dorothy: Where do I find these wonderful machines?

Tinman: My Apple computer can help you. *(Beeping sound effects.)*

Dorothy: Maybe being in Computerland *is* a blessing after all. But I shall have to leave. How can I return to Computerland in Cherry Hill?

Tinman: Just a press of this button on my computer (repeat beeping effects) and—oh, take Two Ninety-Five to Route Seventy. It's right off the ramp!

Dorothy: Oh, I *will* return to Computerland, Cherry Hill. There's no place like home, there's no place like home, there's no place like home.

Computer: There's no place like home for an Apple personal computer. Computerland, Route Seventy Cherry Hill: It's *not* a fantasy!

Analysis: This commercial played upon the listeners' empathy for a well-loved character, plus a familiar archetype—the damsel in distress. It suggested a relatively new idea for its time—computers in the home.

Spot Number 5

Advertiser: Thrifty/Budget Auto Insurance

Length: 60 seconds

Instructions: Young male patient with Austrian psychiatrist.

Doctor: There, there now, tell me about your dreams.

Patient: Doctor, they're not just *dreams.* They're coming *true!* First, I get a cancellation notice from my car insurance company— then I call all these brokers and stay on hold for hours—and I still can't get insurance without paying astronomical rates— doctor, can you help me?

Doctor: Of course! Yours is a common problem with young men. I want to try something. When I say these words, tell me what pops into your head first: thrifty, budget.

Patient: Economical! Save money!

Doctor: Very good. Now, auto insurance —

Patient: Bankruptcy!

Doctor: No, no, my friend—not anymore! Thrifty and Budget mean great savings on auto insurance! And low monthly payments with a small fifteen percent deposit! Repeat after me: In New Jersey, call Thrifty. In New York, call Budget.

Patient: In New Jersey, call Thrifty; in New York, call Budget. Doctor, I'm cured!

Doctor: Not until you make the phone call. Here are the numbers.

Announcer: In New Jersey, 837-6777. That's 837-6777. In New York, 516-555-4670. 516-555-4670.

Doctor: Stop dreaming and start saving! Call Thrifty Brokerage in New Jersey, or Budget Brokerage of New York!

Analysis: We don't recommend two phone numbers. However, the ad costs were split by two brokers serving different territories within the same broadcast area. Some fun things happen with an ad like this. Once in the studio, one of the actors repeated the doctor's line complete with his accent, adding an unanticipated humorous twist. The emotional intensity here builds to a fever pitch. This one has all the elements of a classical drama in sixty seconds—conflict, rising action, climax, resolution, and denouement. Listeners experiencing the same problem as the character responded—enthusiastically.

Spot Number 6

Advertiser: Scerbo Buick

Length: 60 seconds

Customer: Right there guys, thanks. (*Sound of metal dropping*)

Salesman: Uh, ma'am, may I help you?

Customer: Sure, grab that socket wrench (*sounds*)—thanks—this *is* Scerbo Buick, right? Where the man on the radio said you can "build your own Buick." (*Whistles.*)

Salesman: This is Scerbo Buick, and we are running a "build your own Buick" promotion, but—

Customer: Great! They said the new Riviera is about a foot longer? Tape measure, please; right *there*—

Salesman: Wait! When Scerbo Buick advertised, "build your own Buick," they meant look in the book and pick out the options you want. You "build your own Buick" *on paper.*

Customer: Great! Where's that T-square? Triangle, compass—

Salesman: Ma'am, here at Scerbo Buick, all you have to do is tell us what you *want* in your car—*Buick* will build it for you.

Customer: Why didn't you say so? That's easy.

Salesman: Come on in my office.

Customer: Are you kidding? No Buick would fit in *there!*

Announcer: See the new '89s *now*, at Scerbo Buick in Boonton. Scerbo Buick is a Mister Goodwrench dealer. No one knows your GM car better. No one. GM quality service parts.

Customer: Couldn't I just buy one from the lot?

Salesman: (*sighs*) It's going to be one of those days.

Analysis: This ad worked because it allowed the listener to project him- or herself into the situation. Even though a slight exaggeration, it provided a very visual picture of a real-life scenario.

Spot Number 7

Advertiser: Rutland Home Center

Length: 60 seconds

Instructions: Real-life characters; upper-middle-class couple. Outdoor sound effects—birds chirping, distant lawnmower, etc.

Deb: What are you looking at, Jim? Ah, the photo album—brings back memories. Oh, look, remember Davey's first birthday party?

Jim: That was the first time we used this deck. I'll never forget how the guys from Rutland Home Center built that deck. I'm still amazed—first they designed it on a computer; then they picked out premium lumber; had it delivered over fifty miles—

Deb: And the Rutland Home Center crew worked so *fast*—

Jim: It just really made the party.

Deb: Turn the page. Oh, look—Susie's first birthday. What a difference those paving stones made in the driveway—

Jim: Another Rutland Home Center job. Look at Scruffy, in the baby carriage. She was just a pup. Remember, she kept barking at the Rutland Home Center trucks?

Deb: She just wanted a ride. Look at this place. Ever since that first visit to Rutland Home Center, we've just transformed it into a dream house. The Marvin windows and patio doors; the remodeled kitchen—even the kids' swings and slides—

Jim: Even the paint that's waiting for me. There *are* a few things I still have to do myself, but I have to admit, home sweet home got a lot sweeter, thanks to Rutland Home Center.

Deb: Go to it, Rembrandt—I'll start dinner.

Announcer: High quality—not high prices—Rutland Home Center, Route Thirty-one in Clinton. Rutland: Making home sweet home even sweeter.

Analysis: By wrapping all the couple's fond memories around their home improvements, this campaign creates a feel-good impression of the store. It gives the listener a complete sense of what to expect before he or she ever visits the store. It also provides the "big idea" for a series of ads. Furthermore, it takes the store out of the price competition arena. Large chain home centers capitalize on low-ticket "loss-leader" advertising to lure customers in. This campaign plays up the strength of the independent store—its full-service approach to high-ticket home improvements. That brings the store a much better return on its advertising investment, as well.

Spot Number 8

Advertiser: Rutland Home Center

Length: 60 seconds.

Instructions: Same characters as previous spot; early morning; birds chirping, dog barking in background.

Deb: Where are you taking me? Wait—my robe—(*gasps*) where did that load of stone come from?

Jim: Methinks the lady doth protest too much. (*She laughs.*) Rutland. All good things come from Rutland, m'lady. Rutland Home Center—

Deb: You woke me up at six o'clock on Sunday to show me a pile of stone?

Jim: Not a "pile of stone"—L.T. paving stones. Come. Rutland Home Center dropped these off yesterday. Look: *That* pile is going to be our driveway. Imagine interlocking stone in a fish-scale pattern. I drove them crazy at Rutland—ten colors to choose from—you know me. And this stack will go around the pool.

Deb: Am I missing something? We don't *have* a pool.

Jim: Just kidding. These are for the patio I promised you, below the deck. Get this. The guys at Rutland Home Center told me these L.T. paving stones won't peel or flake; no freeze-thaw damage; they're not slippery, and they inhibit moss.

Deb: Made by L.T.? Hmm—colored all the way through— this *was* worth getting up for—if *you* make breakfast, that is.

Announcer: Rutland Home Center, Route Thirty-one Clinton; making home sweet home even sweeter. Rutland paves the way. Stop in.

TOOLBOX

Create advertising that entices the listener, viewer, or reader to want your high-ticket items. It will bring you a better return-on-investment, and take you out of the price war.

Spot Number 9

Advertiser: Clear Eyes Rx

Length: 60 seconds

Instructions: Open with sound effect of cellular phone ringing. Other sound effects as indicated.

Marcia: Sylvia, I'm on the expressway (*traffic sounds*) and the sun glare is *killing* me.

Sylvia: Marcia, darling, I told you to go to Clear Eyes Rx. I'm on the beach wearing my polarized Bausch and Lomb RayBans. No glare here. Just gorgeous hunks in trunks. (*Seagulls*)

Marcia: You mean if I had gone to Clear Eyes Rx, I could lose all this sun glare?

Sylvia: And get 100 percent ultraviolet protection. (*Sighs.*) Speaking of U.V., Sergio, rub a little sun block on my neck, will you?

Marcia: No justice, Sylvia. You've got the hard bodies and I've got bumper to—

Sylvia: Speaking of hard, Marcia, buy a pair of Ray-Ban sunglasses at Clear Eyes Rx; they're coated with amorphous diamond—

Marcia: (*Sighs.*) Diamond. You know all my weaknesses, Sylvia.

Sylvia: Ray-Ban sunglasses from Clear Eyes Rx are ten times more scratch resistant than ordinary glass—Sergio, hand me that glass, the piña colada. Ta ta for now!

Marcia: (*Traffic, horn sounds*) Wait—does this Sergio have a friend? Sylvia? Sylvia? (*fade*)

Announcer: Get to Clear Eyes Rx's sunglass sale now. Get genuine Ray-Ban Survivors—scratch-resistant, glare-reducing, U.V. protected, at Clear Eyes Rx, Route Seventeen Paramus and Route Twenty-Three Wayne.

Analysis: This and several other dialogues between the "princesses" accented the optical industry's efforts to reposition an appliance as a fashion accessory. The retailer succeeded in coat-tailing the manufacturers' marketing strategy.

TOOLBOX

Radio allows the advertiser to create any illusion the listener can imagine; just tailor the setting, the characters, and the message to the station's audience profile.

PRINT ADS

Ad Number 1

Advertiser: J. C. Reiss Optician, Morristown, NJ

Headline: "Why Can't Johnny Read?"

Subhead: "Maybe Because He Can't See the Board."

Visual: Headline was drawn in a childlike manner, as if on a chalkboard.

Body: Have your child's eyes checked, and bring your prescription to J. C. Reiss.

Analysis: This ad ran in the local newspaper for a one-store optical shop. This ad pointed out the importance of a child's visual health when it comes to his or her academic success. The same concept aired on radio, complete with the sound of the school bell. The optician bought into the premise that parents care, and added a little nostalgia—most adults remember their own school days with a certain fondness. A second ad followed, offering "Kidproof Glasses"—durable, with spring-hinge frames, scratch-resistant lenses, and a free breakage warranty.

TOOLBOX

Ad Number 2

Advertiser: Square Luggage, Morristown, NJ

Headline: "We Make a Case for You"

Visual: Photo of a woman's torso with a fashionable briefcase perched atop her legs as she sits on a leather couch.

Body: Refers to her stepping out, prepared to make her case.

Analysis: Mickey Piombo, the owner of this store, cites this ad as producing "the best response of any ad we ever ran." Since this ad ran, his operation has grown from one to four locations.

Once again, this ad proves that you can make a big impact without a big budget. I shot the photo right in my home office, had my wife pose for it, and processed it in my basement darkroom. It appeared in a regional magazine read by upscale career women. The advertiser looked first-class. It also won an award in competition with several major ad agencies submitting work they did for big-budget advertisers.

TOOLBOX

Keep your ads lively; they will die of exhaustion if you try to make each ad do too much. Keep a single, primary focus—announce an opening, new merchandise, new location, larger location, etc.

Ad Number 3

Advertiser: Painten' Place, Denville, NJ
Headline: "Think How Nice It Feels To *Walk* On . . . "
Visual: Man standing on his head, on a carpeted surface.
Analysis: Owner Richard Yobs illustrates the fine art of growing his business—by staying open to his ad counsel's ideas, no matter how outrageous. The ad "jumped off the page" at his customers; many of them commented on it.

For years, Painten' Place was known as just that—a paint store. After about seventeen years in business, Yobs enlarged the store, adding other home-decorating products like blinds and carpet. Just mentioning the new additional merchandise didn't seem to be enough. The customers still didn't realize they could coordinate their other home fashions in Rich's store.

Finally, we proposed something dramatic. He went for it. We actually produced the ad by having the owner standing with a carpet sample on top of his head, taped his necktie to the carpet and pulled his eyeglasses halfway out of his pocket. We simply inverted the photo when we assembled the ad. Although the ad was small, in black-and-white, and surrounded by a page full of other ads, it caused a stir.

Ad Number 4

Advertiser: Floor Fashions, Morris Plains, NJ

Headline: "*Wood* We Forget a Memorial Day Sale? Never."

Visual: Patterns of wood flooring

Analysis: This ad communicated quickly and cleanly, without the usual retail "clutter." It was neither large nor colorful; it didn't even mention a price. But it *did* get your attention— and you know *instantly* what the store is selling.

Ad Number 5

Advertiser: The Original Platforms & Waterbeds, Union, NJ

Headline: If You Bought a Waterbed
(from anyone else)
Bring Us Your Receipt
And We'll Take 20 Percent Off
Their Price.

Analysis: This ad takes advantage of the "buyer's remorse" that often follows a consumer's high-ticket purchase. We knew that a good number of people walked out of a store after making a furniture buy with that gnawing feeling that maybe they didn't get the best price. We offered them a second chance to find out.

TOOLBOX

Combine creative strategies with media strategies that make sense together. Place "off-the-wall" ads in front of "off-the-wall" audiences. Always make them want more.

THE GREAT OUTDOORS

Billboards can also provide a solid medium for your company to advertise on. Below are suggestions if you decide to advertise on a billboard, including an example of a strong outdoor ad.

Advertiser: Storerunner.com

Headline: "One Dot Shopping"

Analysis: Here is an example of a well-executed billboard advertising campaign. Storerunner demonstrates that outdoors, less is more. All that appeared was the headline on top and the advertiser's logo across the bottom.

Outdoor advertising is probably the most abused form of advertising. Too many people just don't know how to design for it. You cannot simply take your newspaper or magazine ad and put it on a billboard.

Consider this: The communications process is different for outdoor advertising. First, you usually view a billboard at a distance. No matter how big it is, from a distance, each of the items on the billboard looks small. Second, the exposure time is generally much shorter than other forms of printed communication. You sit in a chair and read the paper, a magazine, or your mail. You sit in a car *moving at high speed* when you read a billboard.

Like we said before, in the right hands, the right tool can be deadly. In the wrong hands, forget it. Even some of the biggest, best, and brightest ad people simply don't know how to create effective billboards.

TOOLBOX

Run a "progressive" campaign with outdoor ads; change the message, to create a series or to tell a continuing story about your business.

So, what does it take?

Very simply, here are a few rules to make an impact with outdoor advertising. They apply to standard billboards, as well as moving ones, like the ones on buses and trains.

- Less is more.
- Keep the number of items to a minimum.
- The rule of thumb is *nine words or less.*
- Eliminate anything extraneous. If it is not absolutely necessary, don't include it.
- Use high-impact colors: Black and yellow is the highest impact color combination for signage; white lettering on a red background is the second highest.
- Beware of colors that "vibrate" together. This includes complementary colors (those on opposite sides of the color wheel), like red and green.
- Forget the usual design rules. Throw out the arty. Big, bold typefaces rules. *Everything* has to loom large.
- In fact, larger than life is better. Use "monumental" graphics that burst off the board. For example, don't show the person's whole body; just a section of it. The viewer's mind will fill in the rest.

TOOLBOX

Use rotating locations to create the illusion of a larger outdoor advertising showing.

BIG BANGS FROM LITTLE BUCKS

Jeff Witchel, of Witchel Advertising in East Brunswick, New Jersey, says, "Just because your business is small doesn't mean you can't have big ideas."

Jeff should know. He has worked for Young and Rubicam, as well as Grey Advertising, two of the biggest ad agencies in the United States. Today, as a freelancer, he creates world-class advertising for smaller companies. What do the successful ads have in common, even if they run in different media? We asked our expert. Here's what he said.

"You don't need a big budget to have an attention-getting idea that gets noticed, and that sells," Witchel said. He created a campaign that repeated the same visual in each ad for a small, emerging software company. The product provided a breakthrough solution for computer networks. The ads took nine computer monitors stacked up three-by-three, and displayed a NASA shot of the earth. The headline invited the reader to "Turn Your Desktop into a Global Conference Room." At the time, teleconferencing was its infancy.

"The ads produced an onslaught of response," according to Witchel. They used a high impact, powerful, and memorable image, along with a strong user benefit to convince consumers that the long-awaited break-through in network conferencing had finally arrived. How successful was the campaign? The company went from a three person start-up in a two-room office to a global company with over 100 employees in less than three years. Eventually, Insoft was sold to Netscape.

"Such success comes from having a great product combined with an equally great advertising approach. Most importantly, it did not cost a lot of money," he said. Witchel used a free, public-domain photo from NASA, and a single photo of a monitor; the rest was assembled on his computer. "A larger ad agency would have spent much more of the advertiser's money to achieve the same effect," remarked Witchel.

TOOLBOX

Remember, it's not the size of the ad that counts; a small ad with a strong reader benefit or an attractive offer will out-pull a larger, weaker ad.

Saving Artifacts—and Money

What can you do when you have virtually no budget to work with? In 1978, a group of prominent Bostonians tried to save the famous Gilbert Stuart portraits of George and Martha Washington. These works had been on loan to a Boston museum for more than 150 years. The owners had decided to sell the paintings to the National Portrait Gallery at the Smithsonian Institute in Washington, D.C., for $5 million.

"A lot of successful advertising plays on people's emotions," according to Witchel. The solution: "With a series of television commercials, we informed the people of Boston that a piece of their heritage was being sold to the highest bidder." Since Bostonians pride themselves so much on the preservation of their heritage, this approach struck a nerve with them.

A campaign was launched to show what would happen if more of Boston's famous landmarks disappeared. Each commercial simulated how the Boston landscape would change without its familiar monuments. The result: The campaign raised *more than $2.5 in two months.* Here's the kicker: The entire campaign cost only about $8,000 to create. Public service ad time was donated to run it.

TOOLBOX

Today, the average television commercial shot in the United States costs about $300,000. It doesn't have to. Leave the guys and gals home who tell you they need a production unit to powder all the noses. Now, more than ever, you can work wonders and save a lot of money with computerized editing . . . instead of expensive trips to exotic locations.

Let's review what we learned from Jeff:

- "Big ideas start with a strategy that gets inside consumers' heads—one that hits exactly the right nerve to sell."
- "Very often, this involves reaching them at the emotional level—positioning the product as something that will answer an emotional need."

These lessons apply to both consumer and business-to-business advertising. Whether you are selling software or historic preservation, the same principles rule. Whether you want photo processing that gives you great pictures of your grandchildren, or a piece of equipment that makes your business produce wealth, it still involves emotion.

Leave 'Em Spending

What have we learned from this chapter? Very simply, that a good ad is *one that sells*. If it gets results, it's a good ad. If it doesn't, it is not. Don't fall for anything less—or more. Big budgets don't create good advertising. "Artistic acrobatics" don't, either. No matter what medium you advertise in, there are principles that govern what works. Creative is not as subjective as you might think. Your guiding rule should always be: "Does this design element (or do these words) in my ad copy contribute to selling my product?" If not, *get rid of it!*

TOOLBOX

Beware of ad agencies and production companies that insist on the latest technology—on your nickel. I defy the most trained ear to go up and down the radio dial and tell me which commercials were done in a digital recording studio . . . *they can't!* Don't fall for it. Use the level of quality needed to get the result—no more, no less.

◀◀ Time Capsule: "Dine at Teddy's"

Whenever I get the chance to bring a group to Mr. Roosevelt's place, we always have a great time. It's got to have something to do with his joie de vivre. Observe that little knot of people peering into the window, checking out the menu, I'm sure. Let's get closer.

See those envelopes they're clutching? Teddy has a penchant for unique, eye-catching mailings. Let's go in. How novel! Look over at the next table, where they're all opening the envelopes. Chocolate pince-nez glasses, with licorice mustaches—how clever! And the steak knives look just like Teddy's famous sword. I'll bet they'll remember this place. Waiter, was that a horse I just saw ride by the window?

The maitre d' says we can play horseshoes while we wait for our table. Just like Teddy, always keeping the troops entertained. Thank you, sir. The table by the window will be fine.

Check this out . . . that uniformed group of quartermasters and bugle players is going to sing the house specials. A good promoter never stops advertising, even when the patrons arrive.

Pass me one of those envelopes, please. I thought so. Take careful note; those coins inside were freshly "minted" . . . they're after-dinner mints!

Funny thing about this place . . . every time I hear reveille, I think of it; every time I see licorice, I now think of Teddy's mustache—and now I get hungry whenever I pass an eyeglass shop. Excellent use of the subliminal, Roosevelt. ▶▶

The Highlight Zone: "But It Will Never Fly"

Submitted for your approval, a small group of men and women around a table—all advertising professionals, all talking about a new product, all operating in the Highlight Zone.

"We've never done it that way before."

"That's exactly why we should try it this time. There's never been a product like it before. We can't advertise new things the old ways."

"Do you think people will really want to own one?"

"It's our job to convince them of its value and of its usefulness to them."

"What do you think we should call it"?

How about "the telephone?"

The product or service you shelved may now be an idea whose time has come. Tell the world, and you'll know soon enough. Keep it a secret, and you'll never know.

chapter 13

Demystifying Media

I promised you early in this book that we would help you navigate the "media maze." Most small businesses are overwhelmed by the many media choices available to them. I've already shown you with many examples, that almost any advertising medium can get results—if it's handled properly. It's not so much a question of "Which ones work?" or even "Which ones work for my product or industry?" It's more often a matter of which ones will solve your particular marketing problem at a given moment.

I expect that by the time you finish reading this book, you and your advertising counselors will have launched more than one successful new campaign—using at least one or two media you may never have been willing to try before.

But whatever you do, always remember that your media does not operate in a vacuum. It must have a synergy with your creative campaign.

Let's begin to demystify media with the chart below. It will give you a quick overview of some of the best ways to use each advertising medium—a little of the "know when," "know where," and "know how" we discussed in Chapter 4.

Quick-Reference Media Guide

Medium	Best For	Maximize By	For Creative Edge	Couple With
Outdoor	New Product	Point to Location	Minimalism	Radio
Cable TV	Small Trading Area	Buy Multiple Channels	High Production Values	Outdoor, Transit
Spot Radio	Direct Response	Buy Multiple Stations	Big Sound, Low Budget	Outdoor, Transit
Newsprint	Special Event	Multiple Insertions in Same Issue	Benefit-Oriented Headlines	Radio or Cable TV
Transit	Branding	Large Showing	Minimalism	Radio or Cable TV
Magazine	Branding	Editorial Environment	Call to Action	Direct Mail
Direct Mail	Event	Targeted List	Not Junk	Radio or Cable TV

SPECIAL CONSIDERATIONS

The above are not hard and fast rules. The campaign objective and the product purchasing cycle can change everything. For example, a retail auto dealer needs to develop long-term branding and awareness to become top-of-mind with consumers not currently shopping for a vehicle. In addition, the store needs to pique the interest of customers during that brief period when they are in the active shopping mode. This usually only lasts about ten days.

Case in point, if the dealership uses a "pulsing" strategy, the store remains top-of-mind as consumers come *into* the active shopping mode. Remember, pulsing involves keeping a consistent presence with the same audience, then running additional advertising when you have a new product or a special event to promote.

How Long Is Long Enough?

I recently met with a large bank looking to refinance automobiles at more favorable rates for individuals with previously impaired credit.

The ad agency handling their home mortgage business insisted it was not possible to test a radio campaign in four weeks. Wrong. Think again. Let's take a closer look.

As it turns out, the pool of people looking to refinance their car loans is relatively static. They have been in their current situation for some time, and will remain there for anywhere from one to four years. Furthermore, there will not be a great influx of new people entering this prospect pool at any given time.

So we selected several radio stations in a designated city; all of which delivered similar listeners. We then proposed to air the message on all of the stations at the same time, for four to six weeks. Within that time period, if the listeners were both interested and qualified, they would respond.

Following that, the campaign moved to *another group* of stations with an entirely different listener profile. (For example, moving from an English-speaking audience to Spanish-language stations.) By "cycling" through the market in this way, the bank pulled out each group of buyers currently needing to refinance. If the bank stayed on the *same* stations long-term, with this type of product purchasing cycle, the result would be *declining* response levels rather than increasing ones.

Conversely, when a product or service requires a longer decision-making process, the advertiser needs to remain in front of the audience longer. For example, switching brands without a price break or a coupon demands continuous exposure, usually for at least thirteen weeks. (Tests show that awareness peaks after thirteen weeks, with no appreciable increase after that.)

TOOLBOX

When selecting advertising media, consider who buys the product, how often they buy it, and how much you need to sell to realize a return on your advertising investment.

Believe It or Not . . .

When the campaign objective involves gaining credibility, such as with a health care product, a persuasive endorsement by a highly credible physician on both radio and television can turn the tide in your favor—unless he or she does not project well. Once again, take full advantage of the magic of radio's imagination—the doctor will not be judged on the kind of damaging elements that career and image counselors term "deselectors." A soothing voice can carry the message, without the distraction of thinning hair, thickening waistlines, etc.

Protect Thy Good Name

Advertising can also work as a public relations tool. If the ads need to restore credibility lost due to negative press, product liability claims, etc., often the best strategy is to return to the source. One of our clients had been targeted by an investigative reporter, and the story caused his normal 3,000 phone calls per season to dwindle to a trickle. We ran an ad set in editorial style as a reply, right in the same newspaper. The call count increased noticeably.

You may remember the prompt response to the Tylenol product-tampering scare. Advertising addressed consumers with the assurances that the company had addressed the problem, and placed the public's safety at the top of its list.

Maybe you don't think this applies to you. However, all it takes is one negative story in the press to destroy your business. Maybe you think it only happens to large, high-profile businesses. It doesn't. One charge of improper disposal of medical waste can destroy a hospital's reputation. One child hurt at an amusement arcade can chase the crowds away. One abusive employee at a nursing home or a day care center can slam the lid on your business. Worse news: Even if the charge is *groundless,* people still remember it.

So, what's the moral of the story? Address the problem swiftly; get the word out that you've addressed it, but above all, *set the record straight!* While advertising is designed to sell product, public relations involves *creating a favorable climate in which sales can occur.*

Yes, you should consider having a public relations firm available for crisis intervention. However, don't be afraid to put your ad agency to work along with them on this job. The objective is to restore public trust and confidence. The answer is to *use all available means* to get it done.

Mixed Up?

So, if you can make any medium work, why should you buy more than one? Why not just save the money, and buy more inventory? Or take another vacation? There are at least three good reasons for a mixed-media campaign:

No single medium, and no single media outlet, can deliver 100 percent of your target. We live in a fragmented world. Examine the population of Anytown, U.S.A. The young families on one side of town have one lifestyle, and are reached best with certain media; the single people in the apartment complex work and play in a different world; the retirees travel still different paths. You may need to buy newspaper, radio, and cable TV just to reach a high enough percentage of your marketplace to yield a favorable response. Evaluate your trading area and the impact each medium has on it.

There is value to reinforcing your message. Suppose you open your mailbox today and find a circular. Last night, you saw a television commercial for the same furniture store. The circular triggers a recall mechanism that reminds you of the television commercial.

Timing—in life as in business—is everything. You saw the television commercials for the furniture store over a three-month period. You've seen periodic holiday sale ads for the same store in the newspaper. You simply had no need for furniture. Now, after their college graduations, you've decided to convert the kids' rooms into a home office. Voilà—you need furniture! Guess what's in your mailbox?

TOOLBOX

When selecting advertising media, always evaluate whether the campaign is *proactive* (going after customers) or *reactive* (responding to some negative impact on your business). Consider the ability of each medium to respond to time-sensitive issues.

Today, more than ever, these considerations can make or break the success of your ad campaign. We live in a multi-platform world. First, we have seen a convergence of media and media outlets. Your cell phone now delivers your e-mail messages; your cellular carrier and your cable company may be one and the same. Beyond that, entirely new media platforms have arisen to deliver your message. Those new platforms have gained momentum faster than expected.

At the beginning of the year 2000, when the first edition of this book had just been written, I predicted that the brand-new medium of satellite radio would have a similar impact on terrestrial radio to the impact of cable TV on broadcast TV, within a five-to ten-year period. Some laughed. Others paid close attention. Reality set in.

In just these few short years, consumers (yes, your prospects and customers) now have even more media choices. Does that mean you have to buy every advertising medium in sight? Does it mean you should abandon all the traditional media and rebudget all your dollars to newer, emerging media?

Not quite. Here's what it does mean. You and your advertising counsel should keep a close watch on emerging media. At this point, they have not eclipsed all other media. However, certain target audiences—especially teens and younger adult males—are inclined to embrace these new platforms earlier. If these groups compose an important part of your target audience, you need to pay even closer attention to the rapidly changing media landscape.

Even more importantly, we know this: Now that we live in a multiplatform world, it changes the media landscape. As this trend continues, we can expect to find people using both newer and more traditional media side by side. For example, on the commute into work, George will listen to his all-news terrestrial radio station for traffic reports, then switch back to his all-sports station. Once at work, he will listen to his favorite music, which only satellite radio stations play. On the ride home, he will switch to his favorite all-talk station.

PULLING THE TRIGGER

Consider the importance of triggering events that affect your own product or service's purchases. What causes your customers to suddenly come into the market for your product? Remember when we discussed the impact of homes and automobiles on the economy? It's the great aftershock of these purchases that opens wallets, bank accounts, and cash registers.

A single event can easily trigger multiple purchases. The best example is a family moving to a new area. Once they relocate, they need everything from new doctors to new carpeting to a new cable TV service.

Although we have demonstrated that we can make any advertising medium work, each medium does have certain strengths. You should exploit them. By now, with all the examples I've given you, they should be more obvious. Take another look at the chart in the beginning of this chapter. Can you see how you might mount a campaign for your business in one or more media you hadn't considered before?

Try this exercise. Take a sheet of paper. Divide it into columns, using the headings below:

1. Price
2. Product
3. Value
4. Convenience
5. Support

Next, rank the importance of each of these in your business. Then, under each column, list the specific things you do better than your competitors in each area.

Be precise. For example, don't say, "our prices are lower"; say, "We guarantee an everyday price ten percent lower than the lowest-priced competitor."

When it comes to product, specify *exactly* how your product excels. For example, "outlasts any U.S.-made brand in its category." Remember that value is a function of both *price* and *quality.* As for convenience, are you open twenty-four hours a day? Do you have more branch offices than any other bank?

And finally we come to *support*— the missing link that ties together price, product, value, *and* convenience. If you have superior warranties, after-sale service, and replacement/repair, you've got it all. We live and do business in the "service era." Especially in high-paced times and affluent environments, *service is king.*

Why am I even talking about this in a chapter devoted to media? Why didn't I discuss this under marketing, or under copywriting? Fair question.

And the reason is that once you've really gotten down to the nitty-gritty of putting your business under the microscope, only then can you examine what *message* will actually work in each of the various advertising media. Hold that thought.

For instance, if you determine that you absolutely must tell people about this unbelievable warranty program you have, it might just mean you can't be effective in a medium like outdoor advertising, where "nine words or less" is the rule for success. You may require a newspaper ad or a mailing piece to explain the details of your offer.

Yes, often the tail does wag the dog. *Your copy points may very well dictate your media choices.* Got it?

MEATIER MEDIA?

Okay, you've put me against the wall. Now I have to tell you the plusses and the minuses of various advertising media. Keep in mind, I am not saying, "Don't use this or that medium." I am saying use all appropriate media, but use them wisely—for their intended purpose, at the right time. Let's take a magnifying glass to each of them. I'll start with media that people are exposed to primarily in the home.

Newspapers

When I started my advertising career, newspapers were the staple of every small business's ad budget. They swallowed the lion's share of the dollars. Of course, tyrannosaurus rex roamed the earth then.

That was then; this is now. As we mentioned earlier, our society's "time poverty" has since relegated newspapers to a secondary place with most active consumers. As readership continues to decline, so do results.

Once again, this does *not* mean don't use newspapers. It *does* mean you may not be able to use them alone and get the same results in today's world that you would have expected in eons gone by. So, how can we make better use of them?

If you use newspapers today, you need to be aware of how your *customers* use them. People today scan the newspaper *looking for very specific offerings*. If you're going to use newspaper advertising, you must have a strong call to action, usually a price. Keep in mind that if your competitor's price is better, his ad may blow yours right off the page. Aside from that, your ad has to have high-demand merchandise the public can't find anywhere else. Very simply, unless you are content (and capitalized) to build long-term awareness, *don't expect institutional advertising (name-location only ads) in newspapers to produce a quick return today.*

Today's sharper newspaper publishers are addressing declining circulation. *The Wall Street Journal* now has a national network of top radio stations carrying its business reports. Large publishing conglomerates are not the only ones to see and react to changing readership trends. Small-group publishers like W.H. Zerbe of Pottsville, Pennsylvania, saw the light fifteen years ago. This group pioneered a computer-based reader call-in service with advertiser-sponsored audio text messages on a variety of subjects like health, law, sports, etc. Look for progressive publishers offering electronic tie-ins, such as a presence on their Web sites. You have to be where your customers are—and today, *your customers spend less and less time reading.*

Whatever you do, don't fall into the old trap. Your newspaper ad salespeople want you to buy big ads with color. The truth is, results do *not* increase in proportion to ad size—but the *cost* does. It's more important to *repeat your ad often,* even several times, in the *same issue.* That will bring you better results because you have a better chance of readers seeing your ad.

You and your ad agency should negotiate for preferred placement (in a section that your customers are more likely to read), free or reduced color charges, etc. The big bone of contention: Newspapers seldom give you any protection, meaning that they will happily run your ad next to your competitor's ad.

Cable TV

Hey, Martha, I'm gonna be a star! I'm going on TV!

This is how most local cable television is bought—and sadly, how it is sold. Let's shoot a few demystifying arrows into this one. What is cable television? What can it do for your business?

As we said, most cable television is bought for the wrong reasons. Flattering your ego does not grow your business. That said, where, when, and how should you use cable TV?

First, don't buy it because it's cheap, because in most metropolitan areas, it no longer is. If you trade in a wide area, it may cost you more to buy multiple cable systems than it would to buy either a large metropolitan radio station, or possibly even off-peak broadcast TV.

Remember our earlier discussion about when to use television in general? Again, *run your cable TV advertising during the winter months, when people spend more time at home, indoors.* November through March should get you your highest viewership. Run most of your advertising on *evenings and weekends,* unless your product appeals to retirees or stay-at-home parents. It's worth paying the higher rate, since otherwise no one's home to see the ad during the day.

Keep this in mind: Local cable television is *not* rated—the cable company usually cannot tell you how many people are actually watching at any given time. They can only tell you how many *subscribers* they have. Don't buy the argument that people must be watching because they're paying for it. In many localities, especially outlying areas, people subscribe to cable simply because broadcast TV reception is poor. They are, in essence, using their cable TV as an antenna. They may, in fact, be watching *non-cable* programming.

That is not to say that there are no benefits to advertising on cable. Cable delivers your message particularly well when your customers are affluent suburbanites. These areas usually have high cable subscribership.

So, how do you use cable TV effectively?

Besides running your ad at the right time of the year and the right time of the day, you need to be on the right channels. There is a great deal of fragmentation here. How many channels can anyone watch at once? Only one. How many do you need to be on? Several, depending on how broad or narrow your product appeal is. For example, if you sell sports memorabilia, you may only need ESPN and MSG sports channels. However, if you sell aluminum siding, you may need everything from sports channels to movie channels to home and garden channels. Notice these are all plural. Now you know why I said buying cable TV today might not be so inexpensive. *Buying right means buying a lot.*

Great. So, you're going to run on cable TV at the right time and in the right place. What else do you need to do? Well, unless you want the public to see your business as "just another little local guy," you need to invest in a decent creative campaign. This can cost some shekels if you trade in a major metropolitan area.

"Why can't I just let the cable company do my ad?" you ask. "They said they'll do it for only $1,000."

Go ahead, if you want people to *laugh* at your business. I call the typical cable TV commercial a "Hi, Mom" spot—with the owner in front of his or her building, waving like in a home movie. But, if you want them to patronize you, it's worth the investment to produce TV commercials that make your business look like a quality company. Enough said.

Outdoor and Out-of-Home

If you want to pull the captive crowd stuck in traffic, outdoor advertising is a great way to do it. As we said before, keep the message big, bright, bold, and *lean*. But keep in mind that trying to cover all major arteries could prove costly.

In outdoor advertising, brevity is indeed the soul of wit. If your business has a limited trading area, and you want to blanket it, or if you need to pinpoint people in the direct route of travel and lead them to your doorstep, this is a great way to do that, too.

From the standpoint of cost outlay, this may not be the least expensive medium. However, if you measure your media dollars in cost-reach ratios, it is still very cost-effective.

In some areas, especially urban areas, you can buy smaller "junior" billboards. (The industry refers to them as "eight sheet" panels.) Many of these are on the sides of buildings, in parking lots, or at railroad crossings. The advantage: viewers are usually stopped, or traveling at a slower speed, when they see these boards. However, keep in mind that with their smaller size, you have to keep the design and the message even sparser than you would on a larger board.

Don't rule out the many opportunities for transit advertising: bus shelters, taxi stands, bus boards, train platform clocks, train posters, etc. Once again, if you have a wide trading area, this will prove cost-prohibitive.

So you want frequent flyers? Many airports now have displays you can sponsor. Remember, Americans are on the move, and you can *move with them.*

Radio

That's like television, only without pictures, right?

Wrong—they are different worlds. Radio, after all, is *portable.* That's why TV never replaced radio, as some people predicted it would. In fact, radio continues to *grow*—largely because of that portability. As we said earlier, and it bears repeating: Use radio, don't abuse it, and you'll do well.

The good news is that all but the smallest stations subscribe to audience ratings services. Although these are not foolproof, and you still need to know how to interpret them properly, you and your ad counsel can predict—with some certainty—the success of a campaign, knowing the approximate numbers of qualified people you can reach. Larger stations often have more in-depth audience data available as well. They can usually give you qualitative information like listener income, home ownership, educational level, cars owned by the household, etc. For the first time in many years, the radio industry has partnered with advertisers and invested some serious dollars to conduct effectiveness studies. In the era of accountability, everyone wants documented ROI (Return On Investment). See: *www.radioadlab.com.*

Exploit radio's strengths: wide area reach, repetition, local flavor, audience loyalty, exposure close to purchasing time, etc. How do we do this? Sponsor traffic, weather, local news, and other high-attention features. Run customized contests that drive traffic to your door. Get the stations excited about your business, and they'll get the audience excited about it. Create a "deadly" campaign that grabs people by the you-know-whats.

Magazines

Magazines have felt the pinch in recent years. Sometimes that's good, since it means that only the best and the brightest flourish. If your product or service appeals to a real niche market, magazines offer you a highly targetable readership. Also, they have a longer shelf-life than newspapers. Most people keep them around longer, so your ad has a better chance of being noticed—and read—more than once. In addition, magazines offer higher quality reproduction, so that high-quality campaign you created can really shine through. Finally, magazines also have a higher pass-along readership than newspapers. Don't underestimate the importance of this. Many nonsubscribers see your ad in doctor's offices and even auto repair shop waiting rooms.

You don't have to be a national advertiser to use magazines. Some magazines offer regional editions. And, there are some very good regional and small city magazines, as well. When your business needs a high style look, and a certain editorial environment, magazines can provide that.

Direct Mail: Junk vs. Jewels

Literally tons of advertising pours through the U.S. mail every day. You could probably lay a trail across the country with it. A huge percentage of it never even gets opened, let alone read.

Why bother, then? Because every medium has its advantages, as we said before. For one, consumers are used to receiving it. Direct mail doesn't require any learning curve, any new technology, or any change in habits. Everyone goes to their mailbox every day.

Beyond that, direct mail is probably the only medium that can actually deliver *100 percent* household penetration in a given area. Even with the increases in the cost of printing and postage, it has not fallen out of favor. Keep in mind, however, that the average direct mail campaign only gets about a 2 percent response rate, and that's if you mail it solo. When you join other advertisers in a coupon mailer (commonly referred to as "marriage mail"), expect only about half of 1 percent.

So, how do I produce mailings that don't wind up in the trash?

First, it's only junk if they think it is. You need to create the perception that it's not. Make it look important, and give it a quality look. One direct mail company that serves auto dealers has come up with mailings that mimic the look of a special delivery or express mail envelope. They get opened—and read—more often than the average piece.

American Express says that there are three components to a successful mailing:

- The quality of your mailing piece.
- The accuracy of your mailing list.
- The attractiveness of your offer.

As for the quality of the mailing piece, like we've said before, quality sells quality. If your business is a jewel, make your mailing piece a jewel. The investment in better artwork, design and layout, and better printing and paper will pay off. Consumers will more likely open your mailing, read it, and respond to it. They will perceive your business as a jewel, and not as junk.

However, if you're a deep discount warehouse operation, you don't need or want to look fancy. You want to communicate a money-saving business with a money-saving look.

As for your mailing list, *the best mailing piece is useless if the right people aren't reading it.* If you trade in a wide area or solicit mail-order business, you may be more interested in purchasing a list of people who buy similar products to yours, or to people in a certain demographic group (age, sex, income, occupation, etc.), no matter where you live.

Today, mailing lists are available for just about any group of consumers or businesses you can imagine. This helps to assure the targetability of your mailing. For example, if you want male self-employed contractors in selected ZIP codes to see your new line of power tools, you can buy that list—or more accurately, rent it from a list broker. Generally, you have to pay again if you want to use the list again. Some of these lists are compiled from magazine subscriptions; some from deeds and mortgages; others from credit card holders. A legitimate list source will specify their accuracy. If they are updated properly, most lists are guaranteed to be about 93 percent deliverable.

What works in direct mail when you have to be budget-conscious? We asked Sharon Kuflik of Witchel Advertising in East Brunswick, New Jersey, a direct mail specialist. Sharon helped create and carry out successful direct mail campaigns for department store chains like Macy's.

"You can mail whole catalogs cost-effectively if you use third-class mail," she said. "The postage for a catalog would be the same as for a postcard. However, it costs more to produce a sixteen- or twenty-four page piece."

What formats work? "You don't want it to be so small that you get lost in the mail, like a 3- inch by 5-inch postcard," Sharon said. "But, a postcard format, slightly larger, could be very effective. This also saves on the labor it takes to insert a letter into an envelope. It can be very attractive, and the consumer doesn't have to do any work." She finds a stand-alone piece far more effective than a mailing with a group of unrelated businesses.

Kuflik advises would-be mailers to repeat their mailing three times in several months, to be effective. Most importantly, "Do not put ten thousand things on one page; no one will look at it. It's just too confusing."

She suggests that if you are marketing to consumers you should break down your mailing list to the level of one letter carrier's route. In this way, you can address people in a neighborhood where you are already doing business, and are likely to reach similar homeowners with similar needs and interests in your product. This can prove especially valuable if your product targets a high-income group.

Kuflik used this technique successfully for Macy's department stores. "If a neighborhood had ten credit card holders, the other ninety residents would probably be similar in their socioeconomic backgrounds," she noted.

Direct mail practitioners call this "cloning" (and you thought it only worked on sheep!). Suppose you reviewed your sales and found that, although your product didn't necessarily require it, the bulk of your customers seemed to be families with children under age eighteen. Wouldn't it make sense that similar families might patronize you? Can you rent such a list? Of course you can. Send in the clones!

For frequently purchased, low-ticket items, "A throwaway look is okay," she advises. "They're not going to hold onto the mailing for long." However, for once-in-a-lifetime, high-ticket purchases, like a kitchen remodeling job, our expert says, "You want people to believe you are not going to disappear into the night; you want to convey the value of your product. An investment in better paper and design becomes more important. You want them to hold on to it, and nobody's going to hang on to newsprint. It yellows and crumbles."

Is there an exception? Kuflik says there is. When it comes to cars, consumers accept newsprint. The ads are designed to create momentary excitement, and the consumers know it.

What kind of breakthrough techniques can an advertiser use in direct mail? Sharon gives the example of sending a large poster in a tube. It's unusual, and people are more likely to open it. As to sending three-dimensional objects in the mail, like imprinted golf balls, teddy bears, etc., Kuflik expresses mixed feelings.

On the other hand, I have had success with this technique in business-to-business situations. My own ad agency created a "First Ad Kit" to promote itself. It contains items like vitamin bottles filled with candy "pills," Band-Aids, cotton swabs, tongue depressors, etc. Each item has a label attached that extols the virtues of doing business with us. For example, the vitamin bottle bears the label "AdVita: Adds Vitality to Your Ads." The tongue depressor suggests that if you're "depressed about your marketing efforts," call us. People recognize that we got their attention with something unique, and made a positive impact without spending a lot of money. The message is, clearly, if we can do it for ourselves, we can do it for them as well.

TOOLBOX

In direct mail, you want three things: Get it opened, get it read, get it acted upon.

Using the mail in the era of "time poverty" and advertising clutter takes technique. Sharon's advice to direct mail marketers is as follows:

- It has to look interesting.
- The outer envelope should be enticing.
- It has to be short, sweet, and to the point.
- It has to be interesting to read, and appeal to the recipient.
- You must respond quickly to customers answering your mailing.

Here are some "red flags" to watch out for:

More is not always better. If your list broker requires that you purchase 5,000 names, for example, but there are only 3,500 viable prospects, you're paying for both additional printing and postage, when, in all likelihood, you'll get no response from the other people. You're only diluting your response rate. Purchase all of the names, but only mail to the ones you deem productive.

Your mailing piece shouldn't look like junk. It should look like your business is important, and that you are proud of it.

If you do other kinds of advertising, there should be a similar look or message throughout. Your mailer shouldn't look like it was designed on another planet.

Here's the wrap-up: Our expert advises you to refine your mailing list as well as you can; offer something unique—make your mailing piece compelling to get people to look at it. Don't give up; keep trying until you find the right hook.

Above all, *be sure your direct mail piece has a clear call to action, and a user-friendly response mechanism*—a toll-free phone number or a postage-paid reply card.

Among other companies, Sharon Kuflik executed successful direct mail campaigns for Macy's department stores. Each region conducted its own mail-order campaign, inserting "stuffers" supplied by the manufacturers, into credit card statements.

Kuflik noticed that her region was underproducing. The reason? Too many similar offers went out in the same mailing. The solution? She had each merchandise group manager present proposed offers. More diverse offers resulted in more orders—for the same mailing cost. Kuflik was able to identify the items that sold best through phone and mail, and limit the offerings to the more productive merchandise.

In addition, Sharon developed special seasonal books that were distributed both in-store and by mail. Finally, she noticed that in some cases, warehouse personnel simply did not insert the stuffers. As a result of these three simple changes, Macy's New York *doubled* its mail and phone business in six months! Sharon later instituted a mailing inviting Macy's shoppers to come in and register to win a shopping spree. The campaign proved successful as a traffic builder for several reasons:

- It reached out to less active customers.
- It offered a motivating incentive—an attractive prize, like a trip.

- It was repeated, and gained momentum over several years.
- The store placed merchandise on sale, which further enticed customers.
- The mailing had a sense of urgency, since the shopping spree event lasted only one day.
- The mailer required that contest entrants visit the store.

TOOLBOX

Make a breakthrough. Don't resort to cookie-cutter solutions for your next mailing. Think outside the box; expect your direct mail practitioners to do the same.

Entering Another Dimension . . .

6,626,111. Get to know the number. No, it's not the winning lottery number. Ask the U.S. Patent Office what it stands for. Better yet, ask the patent holder.

Harvey Hirsch thought he would retire by fifty-five. The owner of a small ad agency, Hirsch now has to figure out how to get a day off instead. What precipitated the sudden turnaround? Hirsch figured out how to build a better mousetrap. He now holds a patent on his unique process for creating—get this: personalized, full-color, on-demand, three-dimensional mailing pieces.

That's a mouthful. Here's what it means to you. A marketer can pull names at will from a database, target just those leads he or she deems most productive, and mail a three-dimensional piece with the prospect's name all over it—in lots of one, ten, or one hundred.

Harvey has created a whole new paradigm. Instead of paying to print and mail to the 99 percent of unproductive prospects, you can now concentrate on the productive ones. Take this example: Your company has a catalog; 10,000 people have purchased mail-order items from it. You want to get incremental sales from those who have already enjoyed purchasing from you. You cull your list, select the hundred customers who purchased the highest dollar amount in the past year and just mail to them. By sending them a piece with their name all over it, you will get their attention. Now the fun starts. What should you offer them? Not sure? Send the exact same piece with one offer to half of the list, and the exact same piece with a different offer to the other half of the list. Compare the results. Now, send a personalized piece to the 2,000 best customers you have, using the offer that pulled better results.

Although each piece costs significantly more, the increased efficiency of testing, coupled with the increased effectiveness of personalized dimensional mailings, will result in greater profits. Hirsch has used variations of his product line—now consisting of over forty items—very successfully in the business-to-business arena. His clients use his material as appointment-setting vehicles for sales forces. He cites dental labs and office supply dealers as examples of businesses achieving record-setting success levels.

The author conducted an experiment, mailing Hirsch's origami fish design to twenty of the one hundred twenty-five workshop attendees that stayed behind for a book signing. Seventeen of those took his call on a follow-up. That's 85 percent! True, it was a "warm" list—the prospects had some positive prior acquaintance with the person mailing to them, but the number is extraordinarily high.

Suppose you need to really impress just a very few highly influential people to look at your product or service. In the past, traditional printing economies of scale would have dictated a minimum press run of 500 pieces. Even if the design and the copy had explosive impact, in most cases you still only had a flat generic piece going to each person. Now, with today's digital technology, you can produce each piece on-demand (as needed), personalize it throughout (not just where the address appears), create it in three dimensions, and let it keep evolving as your product offerings change.

How far can we take this one-to-one marketing? According to Harvey, as long as we mine the data we control, we already have the ability to create this scenario:

Mr. Jenkins gets on the plane from New York to Atlanta; the airline serves him his favorite fish dinner; when he lands, the rental car agent hands him a box with tickets to the ball game, dry cleaning coupons, dinner reservations at his favorite restaurant, and directions to tomorrow's meeting—all prearranged; all courtesy of his very smart supplier. Do you think they will keep him as a customer for years to come? You can count on it.

Hirsch refers to his breakthrough techniques and his overall approach as "infiltration marketing." You can now initiate and maintain customer relationships with the press of a button. Remember why it works:

- The sweetest sound to many people is their own name.
- "Lumpy" mail gets opened first.
- You only mail in quantity after you have tested.
- You only mail to highly likely prospects with offers that will appeal to them.

What's next in the evolution of the state-of-the-art, you ask? Soon enough, you might open a talking cardboard tube with flashing lights. To really appreciate these marketing breakthroughs, visit: *www.popandfoldpapers.com* and *www.digitaldimensions3.com*.

World Wide What?

I'll bet you were wondering when I'd get around to a serious discussion of Internet advertising. And a serious subject it is. Never has there been anything more confusing to the advertiser than online advertising.

First, keep in mind that *it is not yet a perfect science.* Although Internet access has proliferated, and its penetration rate into the population has rocketed, there are still pitfalls to watch out for.

The biggest single obstacle to advertising on the Internet is lack of standardization. Everyone's radios and television sets are manufactured to receive the same bands and the same frequency ranges. Not so with everyone's Internet. One group of users continues to use 56K modems; others have ISDN, T1, or DSL phone lines. Oh, by the way, did I mention cable modems and fiber optics?

The different technologies all allow different *levels* of access. If your Web site or your online ad features streaming audio or video, some users may not be able to download it properly. Grainy, herky-jerky images do not help to sell your product.

Then there's the issue of software. If users don't have a program such as Adobe Acrobat, they may not be able to view all those beautiful graphics. In short, "your Internet is not my Internet."

So, do we sit back and wait for standardization? Of course not. We try to use the Web the same way we use other media—by targeting our best prospects. Hopefully, these are people that keep up reasonably well with the constantly changing technology.

But remember, the Internet as a communications medium is still being perfected as you are reading this. I spoke to the Interactive Advertising Bureau (IAB). In the year 2000, they had very little industry data to offer to the public. By the end of 2005, that had changed.

Greg Stuart, president of the IAB, discussed the extensive research conducted by the Starch organization, in order to determine the role of each medium in today's marketing plans. The results point to sound advice. However, these studies do reflect tests on behalf of large, well-funded brands. Just a word of warning—the cost of testing ads on the Internet—as well as the cost of running them effectively—may still prove prohibitive for many smaller businesses.

The IAB claims that only one of every five ads tested well. What do we look for? According to Stuart, many ads don't pass the "glance test" (the first three seconds)—they don't communicate quickly enough for consumers who just don't stick around long enough. So, rule number one for online advertising: *Say It Fast.* Get to the point; avoid long setups.

Stuart cites the second most frequently made mistake in Internet advertising: The brand must be immediately recognizable and must appear throughout the ad. Third, the message must motivate. Hey, this sounds strangely like traditional media. You got it. What works, works . . . both online and offline.

So, where are the "budget stretchers" for the smaller company trying to advertise online?

Stuart advises:

- Invest 10 to 20 percent of the total budget in online advertising.
- Use so-called "rich media" ads (those with animation programs like Macromedia or Flash perform at triple their cost).
- If possible, cut out advertising that will go overseas.
- Optimize your Web pages, so they come up more often in searches.
- Don't overinvest in your company's Web site. Only 20 percent of consumers go directly to a corporate Web site.

Like every other medium, we posed the question of trackability. The IAB advises:

"There is no relationship between click-through (from banner ads, etc.) and brand attitude change. However, sales from interactive advertising are highly trackable." He cites cases like Ford Motor Company, where companies shifted dollars into the medium and compared their sales. Stuart cites a study indicating that Colgate toothpaste would have missed 26 percent of its purchasers if all the dollars went to television alone. Similarly, he points to McDonald's, stating that the fast food marketer would have missed six million consumers if it did not include online advertising for the introduction of a new menu item.

So, how does the smaller advertiser use the Internet most effectively?

- Use search engines first. Those consumers using them are four times more likely to purchase.
- Use e-mail by building a solid list.
- Advertise on Web sites relevant to your brand.

The real power of the Internet lies in its synergies with other media. The IAB's Stuart agrees, stating "The Right Mix Rules." During the late 1990s, when the Internet bubble burst and the great shakeout occurred, only those Web-based companies that could turn a profit survived. At that time, business reporters observed that the most profitable Internet advertisers were those brick and mortar businesses with an online component.

I found people at rep firms that sell online advertising networks (advertising on bundles of sites) helpful, spelling out these ways to use the Internet to advertise your business:

Banner ads. These are the long ads across the screen when you first access a site. They must communicate quickly. They must also download quickly. The rule of thumb is eight seconds. If it takes longer than that, you've lost people. Take note: On average, *only about 2 percent of all Internet users actually read banner ads.* Take double note: *Only three-tenths of 1 percent of all users actually click through*—that is, open up the banner ad for more information, or hyperlink to your home page. That said, you better *reach at least 100,000 users in a month,* in order to see any kind of response. (As always, response rate is also a function of how attractive your offer is.) If you're going to create banner ads, make 'em bold and easy to read. There are banner exchange programs that allow you to place a banner on someone else's site; in exchange, you place their banner on your site. Just be sure there are no ethical or industry conflicts before you enter into these arrangements.

Pop-ups. These are the smaller ads that appear on Web sites or search engines. Yes, people have become jaded about them. But piling on animation and detail will *not* increase your click-through rate.

Targeted e-mail. Several companies offer free e-mail, in exchange for collecting data on the e-mail subscribers. This allows them to sell an "online mailing list" to interested advertisers. More sophisticated e-mail companies like Mail.com can actually sell you an e-mail program that isolates recipients by industry, by company size—even by job title. *Wall Street Journal* network radio reporter Joe Connolly reports they get better response rates than banner ads.

Your Web site. But what do you want your site to do? If it is strictly informational, you may be able to get away with just scanning and posting your brochure. However, if you're looking to conduct e-commerce—if you want people to actually *buy* during their visits to your site—that requires a whole different level of commitment to the Web. Yes, you can go out and buy off-the-shelf software and build your own Web site, but once again, we advise that you don't try this at home. If you're serious about doing business online, hire a qualified Web developer. Admittedly, that's easier said than done. With a science this new, whom can you trust? Ask someone at a company with a well-constructed e-commerce site who built it for them. A Philadelphia beverage company hired a Temple University student to put up a Web page. Just one problem—at the close of the school year, the student went back to Germany!

Reality check: *Internet advertising is not cheap.* If you measure advertising costs in terms of cost-per-thousand people reached, as most advertising media do, Internet costs often range from $30 to $200 per thousand—compared to an average local newspaper CPM (cost-per-thousand) of $10; an average local radio CPM of $5; and a network radio CPM of about $2 to $3.

It's your wallet. Once again, that doesn't mean the Web shouldn't be a part of your mix—if you can afford it, and if it has a high likelihood of performing for you, taking into account the user base.

E-commerce reality check: I attended an e-commerce seminar not long ago. One of the panelists operated an online catalog company with high-quality, upscale, unusual merchandise. She indicated that her company had *spent two years and more than $600,000 to develop the site*, prior to launching it!

Does that mean you can't succeed on the Web without a mega-investment? No, but to quote Richard Bienvenue, owner of Foteck studios in Baton Rouge, Louisiana, "You get what you pay for. In the 1970s, anyone with a 35mm camera was a 'professional photographer'; today, anyone with a laptop thinks he or she is a webmaster. Small businesses should go with the best Web designers they can find—or they risk having a very unprofessional image on the Web." Richard goes on to advise looking for a turnkey operation that takes full responsibility for their work. The alternative is "finger pointing": i.e., it was the designer; it was the engineer; it was the photographer's fault, etc.

How do you separate yourself from the spammers—those dumping tons of unwanted e-mail that simply gets deleted without ever being read? The IAB's Greg Stuart advises:

- Permission rules: Make sure you get people's approval to include them on your list.
- Good headlines matter (author's no.te: like any medium, benefits, benefits, benefits!).
- Be respectful of people's privacy.

Can you make money on the Web? Certainly, people are doing it every day. What then, does it take? Besides hocking your eye-teeth or raising money with an IPO, you need these elements to succeed:

- An easy-to-remember and easy-to-find URL, or domain name for your site. If they can't remember it, they surely will not go there. People are paying record amounts of money just to buy out a catchy name that someone else had the foresight to register.
- A site that downloads quickly, is well organized and easy to navigate, offers useful information, is updated often, and asks for the order.
- Your site must also give assurances of reasonable *security* for online transactions, and have a good mechanism for *data capture*, to allow you to follow up inquiries from prospects not ordering yet.
- A *good online advertising campaign* that brings Web surfers to your site by means of banners, hyperlinks, etc.
- A high-profile *offline advertising campaign* that burns your domain name into the public consciousness. Very few e-commerce companies have succeeded without a significant offline campaign to drive traffic to their sites.

Use any and all appropriate and affordable traditional media to make your Web site "rock." Otherwise, kiss it goodbye; it's just a billboard floating in cyberspace.

Finally, if you've hired a competent Web site developer, he or she will take all the extra steps to make sure your site gets the hits you need—including registration with major search engines, creation of "meta tags" (hidden description codes that search engines see), and other devices to make your site rise above the growing Internet clutter. Just as with any other media, use everything at your disposal. Create an online newsletter, join newsgroups (online discussion groups), hold contests—anything to draw attention to your site and your company. Next time you sign on, visit *www.IAB.net.*

TOOLBOX

> Internet Success Formula: Get 'em to your site; keep 'em there; get 'em back; get 'em to refer others.

What have we learned? There is no mystery in media selection. Remember, each medium has a time, a purpose, and a place. Use it for its intended purpose; exploit its strengths; and also use the different media together for maximum impact. The synergy of a mixed-media campaign with a creative campaign that "translates" from one medium to another can blow the doors off your competition.

The Highlight Zone: "Remember When . . . "

Submitted for your approval, a world where the media controls every thought and every act, making it a crime to think anything you didn't read, see, or hear in the mass media.

Far-fetched? Not in the Highlight Zone.

You wake to a robotic alarm clock that someone else set. It tells you what to wear, how to adjust your thermostat, who is running for the local school board—and where and when you must vote for them.

In your car, the same robotic voice tells you where to drive, and at what speed. When you get to your office you hear the same voice announcing the company's takeover—and whether you still have a job.

When the day ends, your car takes over, reminding you what errands to run and what to pick up at the store.

You arrive home to watch the evening news, and realize what's missing. You miss all those old-fashioned, catchy jingles, slogans, and sponsorships. Remember when you actually got to pick out which brand you wanted? The ads were more fun than the programs! Wake up. You were dreaming. Weren't you?

chapter 14

Think You Can't Afford Advertising? Try These Budget Stretchers!

Help! I just can't advertise everywhere, all the time. What can I do to make enough of an impact? How can I stretch my dollars, without spreading them too thin? Relax, and I'll tell you.

NEGOTIATE, NEGOTIATE, NEGOTIATE

First and foremost, let's talk about negotiating with the media. Even though they will tell you the rate card is firm, something is always negotiable. Listen to tapes by Roger Dawson or Herb Cohen, or read their books on this subject. Their premise is that everything is negotiable—even when they say it's not.

Let's get real. Can you expect something for nothing? Maybe, depending on how much of something you're *already* buying, or how badly the media wants or needs your business. So, what should you expect to be able to negotiate?

For the most part, newspaper rates have seldom been negotiable, unless you are a *huge* advertiser buying *tremendous* amounts of space. However, while rates may not be negotiable, other considerations are. For example, I have seen advertisers and ad agencies negotiate free color or preferred positioning. Do not underestimate the importance of what page you appear on, or where you appear on the page. Placement can determine whether your ad is seen or not.

Historically, radio and television rates have been highly negotiable. In recent times, as demand for radio has heated up, that negotiability has begun to wane. However, once again, *you* may not be buying enough to negotiate more favorable rates, but your ad agency or their media buying service (an outsourced media department) may. My rates are often based on a history of buying from stations and networks. As a result, even when the demand heats up and the market gets tight, and even with increases, my rates are usually still better than my clients could have gotten for themselves. It's called "grandfathering."

Part of "know-when" involves knowing when the media is "soft"— when they may be slower, and more inclined to offer deals. Typically, in most markets, radio experiences less demand during the first and third quarters. Listenership does *not* decline, making it an attractive media buy if costs do decrease. However, even the traditionally slow periods have experienced higher demand in recent years. Of course, there are exceptions. Resort areas may have a different seasonality, for example. Television, on the other hand, is slower in spring and summer months; but be careful, because viewership *does* decline during these periods. You get what you pay for.

Here's one brilliant opportunity for a local advertiser: Media Networks Inc. (MNI), a Time-Warner company headquartered in Stamford, Connecticut, offers local advertisers a chance to run an ad in a limited geographic area of certain national magazines. Only the subscribers in certain ZIP codes have your ad bound into the magazine. Can you imagine your customers seeing you in *Time, Newsweek, Sports Illustrated, US News & World Report?* They have no idea the rest of the country hasn't seen the ad. This provides a tremendous prestige vehicle for a small business, in its local trading area. These ads are sold only in full-page size, ranging in cost from about $2,000, depending on the size of the market selected. (This buys you an ad in each of four top magazines.) MNI offers twenty-nine different publications in each of 300 markets around the United States there are fifty MNI offices, nationwide. Check *www.MNI.com* for the one nearest you. Here again, it makes sense to invest in an equally high-impact creative campaign.

"Insider" Trading

A great deal of media cost fluctuations still depend upon timing and personal relationships. I used to place my jewelry store client's Christmas season advertising in February or March, long before the rates increased. This saved them thousands of dollars. In addition, look for ad agencies that are on a short list and get insider deals not offered to general agencies. For example, I have been able to offer some extremely opportune media buys to my clients. These have ranged from as little as $10 to $100 a minute on New York radio—the number-one market in America, where the going rates average about $500 to $1,000 a minute. Have a staff member call around discreetly to the media for rate quotes. Compare your findings with what the agencies are offering. If they place in volume, they should have deals.

One of my clients had been negotiating with a radio station before we began to handle his advertising account. A large amount of money was on the table. Station management was playing hardball with him, sensing that he was extremely anxious to work with them. Midway through negotiations, he called me. We counseled him to temporarily withdraw the deal from the table, until the station met him halfway. The advertiser did not realize it, but he was, in fact, in the driver's seat. He took our advice. As a result, he got more commercials for less money. Always know when to walk away.

In recent years, several companies have experimented with new ways to buy media. While the concept of buying "remnant" space or time (purchasing unsold advertising inventory at the last minute, for reduced rates) has been around for a long time, there are a few new twists to it. One Web site, *www.Bid4Spots.com,* has created a "reverse auction," where advertisers and their ad agencies can go to the Web site, post their parameters (budget, time slots, target demographic) for a given city, and watch radio stations bid against one another. The upside is that the competitive marketplace will drive your costs down. The downside is that the advertiser only has access to participating stations. In order to jump into this game, the advertiser must submit a completed commercial in advance and must pay in full (by electronic fund transfer) prior to the campaign airing—which occurs the week following the auction.

Wanna Take It Outside?

Although billboard companies don't want you to know it, outdoor advertising often has some rate negotiability as well. Even though available billboard space has declined in some areas, decreased supply has not necessarily resulted in cost increases, due to decreased demand. Social and legal pressures are forcing advertisers to withdraw cigarette and alcohol ads. The companies have to make up these lost revenues.

Take a look around your trading area. If you see a lot of donated public service billboards, blank billboards, or "flagging" (torn posters), then conditions may be ripe for you to make a deal. Once again, some ad agencies that place a lot of outdoor ads will have special deals offered to them. Find out whether your agency is on the short list to get these deals. Since the billboard company's rates include the agency's commissions, it doesn't cost you more to go through the agency—and it may cost you less.

Other Budget Stretchers

You can get creative with creating an ad, but you can also get creative with *scheduling* your ads. If your dollars don't permit a daily ad schedule, run alternating days or weeks. The public doesn't know you skipped a day. They only know they keep seeing or hearing you. Over the long haul, you will still establish a consistent presence.

I have done this many times in different media, with good results for my clients. If you run in two different publications, or on two different stations, run one on odd days, and the other on even days. That way, you still have daily coverage.

I told you earlier that increasing ad size does not result in a proportionate increase in results. However, it does increase your costs. Consider running a more consistent, but smaller print-ad presence. Increase the ad size when you have a sale, a special event, or a new product to announce.

Same Time, Same Station?

What about ad lengths in electronic media? Good question. Local spot radio has gravitated to a standard unit of sixty seconds. In most cases, they will charge you 80 to 90 percent of the minute rate to buy a half-minute of advertising. This doesn't make good economic sense for you. This evolved in an effort to reduce the number of commercials. Stations are discouraging thirty-second commercials because the listening audience perceives a unit of advertising as another minute, even if it's only a half minute.

Another thing to consider is that most radio stations still offer some degree of separation for competitive advertisers. In 2005, Clear Channel Communications, the largest operator of radio stations in the United States, broke ranks with tradition and began pushing the thirty-second commercial on local spot radio. The initiative became known as "less is more." The effectiveness of the shorter commercial holds up; the value proposition has come under fire. (We pay more; we get less.)

National network radio has made the thirty-second spot the standard. In networks, a half-minute does actually cost half the price of a minute commercial. As long as you can get your message into thirty seconds, it is more cost-effective for you. You can buy twice the advertising that way.

Television, on the other hand, has been less sensitive to the advertising "clutter factor," and to the viewing audience's concerns. TV has moved from thirty-second commercials to ten- and fifteen- second ads. Interestingly, studies prove that a ten-second TV spot scores about 50 percent of the recall of a thirty-second ad. Just be sure to compare costs.

TV, like newspapers, has little regard for its advertisers. They will often run direct competitors back to back with one another.

Here's a little-known secret in media circles: You can buy ten-second commercials in some very high-profile national network programs, like TV game shows, for a fraction of the thirty-second rate. These are offered mostly on broadcast TV, not as much on cable. The best news: They are scheduled "in program"—not between shows. This gets you a highly captive and often very loyal audience.

Take note: This is not for the faint of heart—or wallet. While the numbers may look heavy to a smaller business, the cost is still far below traditional national television buys. For example, buying this way allows an advertiser to spend $50,000 a week and look as big as a $250,000 a-week advertiser. There are several brokers that offer this opportunity. I recommend PIC-TV in New York.

TOOLBOX

If you are able to afford TV advertising, follow it with a radio campaign that echoes the TV creative. The phenomenon of imagery transfer kicks in. People will hear the radio ad and see the TV ad replaying in their heads.

Co-operative What?

There is a vast advertising resource available to both retailers and wholesalers called co-operative advertising. Many manufacturers offer it. Co-op advertising, as it is called, involves a local business running ads that feature their suppliers' products, with part or all of the ads paid for by the supplier. In most cases, the amount of co-op ad money available to the local business is based on a formula tied to the amount of product purchased. As you buy more merchandise, you earn more advertising funds. These are referred to as "accruals."

What can you do with them, and how do you find out about them? There is no single rule on co-op. Each company has a different policy on how much they will allow, and under what conditions. There are source books full of co-op information. Either your ad agency or your media salespeople should be able to access them for you. Standard Rate and Data Service (SRDS) has published one for many years. You should know that co-op policies are also subject to frequent change.

Let's look at a few details regarding co-op. First, if you buy your merchandise directly from the manufacturer (you take drop-ship deliveries), it is easier to access your co-op. Many manufacturers actually print your accrual (allowance) on your invoice. Otherwise, you should be able to find out how much co-op you have from your sales representative or from the manufacturer's advertising department.

TOOLBOX

One of the best advantages to using co-op advertising involves the small business's ability to coat-tail national and regional ads placed and created by large manufacturers. This often results in instant credibility, immediate identity, and a better campaign than many small businesses can afford to create on their own. To the consumer, you are the local outlet for their favorite nationally advertised brand.

If you buy product through a distributor, different rules apply. Some companies will let the distributor decide how to disburse the funds. Often, a distributor will put an ad campaign together on behalf of a group of retailers. The theory is that a stronger campaign will result than if the individual dealers each placed their own ads. There is a lot of truth to this. The latter often results in a patchwork of ads in different media, and does little to advance the brand within the trading area.

What kind of co-op rules are there? First, most companies do publish an actual co-op advertising policy. This not only makes it easier, but fairer. You should know that the law has ruled on the side of equality here. The Robinson-Patman Act states that, "What they do for one, they must do for another." Keep in mind, however, that the other paint store down the street may have gotten more advertising money because they bought more product than you did.

Companies are allowed to specify how you use the co-op dollars. They may only approve certain advertising media; they may require you to run ads they prepared, or get prior approval on ads you or your ad agency produce. Hint: Don't alter the manufacturer's logo or trademarks, or change their color scheme—you'll never get approved that way!

The co-op policy often specifies when the ads must run, and how soon they must be submitted for credit. Nearly all of them require proof that you ran the ads, as well. Some of them even run the ads through a clearinghouse, such as the Advertising Checking Bureau, to process your claims for reimbursement. Some companies deduct your co-op dollars from the invoices you owe them for product, after you submit bills for the ads you ran. Other companies actually issue a reimbursement check.

If co-op processing sounds onerous, it often is. Don't throw your hands up. Millions of dollars go *unspent* each year. It's "use or lose." If you don't use the money, the next guy or gal will. There are even co-op programs that are 100 percent paid by the supplier! I have seen a few companies, such as Kodak, pay *over 100 percent* for a special seasonal promotion. There have been a few co-op plans that were not tied to purchases—"50-50 unlimited," for example, where the manufacturer pays half of *any and all* approved advertising.

Certain industries are especially co-op friendly. Over the years, I have seen home improvement manufacturers and auto parts and supplies companies dole out quite a bit of money. You will be amazed to find that everything from eyeglasses to fertilizer to cruises is co-op-able.

Is it worth all the time and effort to do some research? You bet it is! The trick is to get your ad people to help you do it. How much advertising money have *you* lost? Better yet, how much could you increase your ad budget if you took full advantage of co-op dollars?

One of my clients used his co-op to leverage his product-buying power. His principal supplier of consumer electronics was slow to process his co-op invoices. His calls went unanswered. When the sales representative noticed the retailer's orders had dwindled, he finally showed up at the store. Harvey had simply switched to another brand of tape decks—buying them from a company that respected its own co-op policy.

Is co-op advertising negotiable? Not often, but occasionally. It pays to ask. If you are a significant player buying a lot of product, or if you opened up a new territory for your supplier, there are often additional unpublished discretionary funds. Some companies have money set aside just to help new accounts, an "opening allowance." The rule here is, if you don't ask, you don't get. For several years, one of my clients tapped into a wellspring of co-op from a vacuum cleaner company.

Vendor Bender?

This brings us to a similar and related topic—vendor support. Whereas co-op advertising is an ongoing situation with most companies, vendor-supported promotions are special events and limited-time promotions paid for in part or in full by a manufacturer—at their discretion. Unlike co-op, there is usually no published policy on vendor support. It comes and goes. The only way to find out about it is to make a proposal to your supplier. Know this: They will be highly selective.

To succeed in getting vendor support, you must first approach the person with the authority to approve it. Very often, this means reaching up to the regional vice-president, or higher. You must demonstrate a clear benefit to the supplier's company and show that you are proposing something not achievable any other way. I have seen "vendor fairs"—mini in-store expositions with manufacturer's representatives conducting product demos—approved for vendor support.

All Together Now . . .

On a similar and related note, there is only so much any one business can do. There *is* strength in numbers, however.

One way to stretch your budget is to do group advertising. There are several ways to do this. First, you can approach your supplier (manufacturer or wholesale distributor) and ask them if they have any organized group ad campaigns planned. If not, ask them to consider one. Second, you can approach other noncompetitive businesses in your community and organize your own share-cost campaign. Third, there may be such an opportunity already organized by your local chamber of commerce, or even by some of the advertising media.

As always, there is an upside and a downside to this approach. First, you will almost always encounter some politics within the group. Second, you will lose some identity. However, in a group situation, you can almost always become part of a much higher profile ad campaign than you could ever afford on your own. The best solution: Run what you can afford to run individually, and supplement that with some group advertising efforts.

I worked at one ad agency where we coordinated an ad campaign for an auto parts dealer group through the warehouse distributor that supplied them. Each month, every dealer got point-of-purchase materials, including window posters and shelf talkers. In addition, each month, we placed them in different media—direct mail, radio, newspapers, and cable TV. Economies of scale paid off. None of them could have mounted a campaign of that prominence or of that caliber by themselves.

TOOLBOX

Buck the tide, and take the bull by the horns! Turn your competitors into your allies by calling a meeting and pulling a dealer group together. Advertise aggressively as a group. If your locations are spread out, consumers will patronize the dealer nearest them. You'll each get your fair share, but the campaign will be much more prominent than anything you can do individually. Divide your ad costs among the group . . . then divide them again, with your common supplier.

Still feel you can't afford enough advertising to do the job?

Your Car

Many small businesses miss good opportunities right under their noses. I have always found that "necessity is the mother of invention"—if you have to, you'll find a way. Consider this. You drive your car all over town. Lots of people see it, day after day. Why shouldn't you use your car to advertise your business? You can put inexpensive magnetic signs on either side. (Don't worry; you can take them off when you go to that wedding at the country club.) Vanity license plates may also be well worth the extra cost. They're cheap when you consider the number of impressions you can make, all year long.

Their Cars

I worked for a radio station that gave their advertising salespeople leased cars with the station's call letters prominently painted on the sides. Give me a car, and I'll advertise for you. What about your staff?

How about the rest of the world? When your product has a cult-like following, your customers will take up the banner. Consider printing bumper stickers. For a few cents each, if there is some incentive or a special affinity between your brand and your customers, they'll put one on. Radio stations do it all the time—"put this sticker on your car; if you're spotted and you hear your license plate number called out on the air, call back and win." Can *you* do this?

Imagine all those moving billboards with your company name, riding around town, and staring your competitor in the face when he or she is stopped at a traffic light! It's worth it! How about cosponsoring a bumper sticker with the local radio station? Coca-Cola and McDonald's have done it. You can, too.

Your Clothes

What about your clothes? Imagine how much additional advertising you could get every time you walk into the bank, the supermarket, or the dry cleaner, if you wore a shirt or a jacket emblazoned with your company name.

It doesn't fit your style of dress? How about a patch on the pocket of your blazer, or even a lapel pin? I used to walk the streets with a button that read "Ask Me For An Idea." People stopped me and did just that. I replied with, "Tell me about your business." It's a conversation starter. It works.

Their Clothes

What about everyone else's clothes? Once again, if your business has a certain cult-like following, people will wear T-shirts, sweatshirts, caps, etc., with your name. If not, give them an incentive to advertise for you. The next time the March of Dimes does a walkathon in your community, sponsor it, and get your name on all those walkers' T-shirts!

Here again, hook up with your local radio station, cable provider, or newspaper. Find out if they're selling or giving away wearables. If you're an advertiser, try to work out a cosponsorship. Offer to pay a small portion of the cost in exchange for getting your name on these items. Keep smiling, because it keeps getting better.

Don't forget that little ad you carry with you every day—your business card. Yes, but how many of them can I hand out? I'm not going to drop them out of an airplane, am I? Well, Joe Girard, listed in the *Guinness Book of World Records* for selling more cars than anyone, and author of *How to Sell Anything to Anybody*, describes how he used to attend local high school football games and throw a fistful of business cards into the air when the home team scored a goal. Believe it or not, some of them found their way back to Joe—in his new customers' hands!

The Road Less Traveled

There are other media solutions, besides traditional mainstream media—and even the so-called new media related to the Internet. Just keep in mind that for most of us in business, these should supplement, not replace, other media.

P.I., and Home Shopping Channels

P.I. (per inquiry) refers to an ad campaign where you only pay based on actual responses to your advertising. Hey, that sounds great! Why don't I just do that with all of my advertising? Here's why.

Per-inquiry ads are used as a way to liquidate unsold advertising space and time. In a good economy, there's not much of that. For the most part, when you see the Ginsu Knife ad on late-night television, that's a P.I. campaign. It does work, but there's a limit to how much P.I. advertising you can get.

Several companies specialize in setting up P.I. campaigns. Most of it is done on fringe TV time and stations. Occasionally, you may find print or radio P.I., but not often. When you do, rest assured your ad will not air or circulate in major outlets in top markets.

Can you make money with P.I. advertising? Yes, you can. Usually, the P.I. company works out a split among all the players—the advertiser, the TV station, and itself. The advertiser also pays a modest fee to produce a commercial, if they don't already have one.

What about home shopping channels? Yes, they are viable; yes, they move product; no, you don't have to pay much up front. Will they accept your product? Get in line. My clients have told me about eighteen-month-long waits for QVC to review and consider their product for possible acceptance. If you're Joan Rivers, that's different!

Per-inquiry advertising and home shopping channels are *not* a substitute for your own properly planned and executed ad campaign—where you control when your ad runs, where your ad runs, who sees it, how many people see it, how often it runs, and what results you get. Use these items as an adjunct. The real advantage is that you may be able to build some brand recognition with both the trade and the public before your product gets into distribution—without incurring much up-front cost.

Up, Up, and Away

Don't ignore peripheral media opportunities—as an add-on to your regular advertising campaign. Earlier, we told you about the Philadelphia furniture stores that flew balloons in the sky. Hot-air balloons, skywriting, airplanes with trailers flying over beaches and stadiums, and blimps can all command high attention from captive crowds. They can also provide a lasting and memorable impression for your business.

Barry Herman, of Barry Herman Entertainment in Livingston, New Jersey, reported this experience: He flew an airplane with a trailing banner over a huge crowd assembled for a Fourth of July fireworks display. Two years later, people still remembered the stunt—and even thought he repeated it annually, although he did not.

What's the secret here? Don't fly a balloon at the Ballooning Festival, where yours is just one more face in the crowd. Do it at a time and place where people *don't* expect to see it.

THE ULTIMATE SOLUTION TO YOUR ADVERTISING NEEDS—YOU

Who are you, really?

I don't mean your name, your occupation, your status; I mean what role do you play in the grand scheme? When you figure that out, you'll know how you can best advertise *yourself.*

Why is this important? Because, *to your customers, you are your business.* How you live, what you give out, and what you give off, are an advertisement. When you advertise yourself, you advertise your business. Whenever Dave Thomas of Wendy's appeared anywhere in support of adoption, people felt better about Wendy's the fast-food restaurant chain—not just about Dave Thomas.

Promote yourself, your business, and your business culture. Every time you appear to present a check to a charity, to flip pancakes at the Rotary Club breakfast, to cut a ribbon, etc., you are promoting your business, as well.

So many of us worry about what people are going to say about us after we are dead. But what are they saying about us now, while we're alive? You are potentially the best—or worst—advertisement your business will ever have. Only you can create this ad campaign. Start now, and good luck.

chapter 15

Promotion: How to Create Larger-Than-Life Advertising

So, you're committed to creating a great advertising campaign. You and your ad agency have done your homework (the market research) and identified the right target audience that buys your product. You've done the media research and found the media that delivers that audience best. You've invested in devising and executing the best possible creative campaign to attract their attention.

But you're still not getting the kind of dramatic response that I've described in this book. Now, what? Jump off the Empire State Building? The Sears Tower? The Eiffel Tower? No. Climb to the top of the tower—and stay on top, by creating a promotion.

Promotion involves taking advertising one step beyond brand awareness and brand preference, and *giving that extra incentive* for consumers to come to you. Promotion is the magic fuel that drives traffic. Sometimes it involves a discount or a coupon; sometimes it involves a prize drawing for winnings. But whatever form it takes, promotion is larger-than-life advertising.

What additional elements do you need above and beyond our persuasion equation success formula in Chapter 5, to make a promotion work? The following covers the elements of a successful promotion.

Speak Directly to Your Audience

For example, if they are retirees and seniors, your prize offering has to appeal to them. It should be something they would want to buy on their own, but either don't have the money for, or maybe something they just never got around to treating themselves to. If you're addressing working women, offer them a day at the spa, or some other stress-reliever. As for our young tech-head friends, maybe they'd like to win free lifelong Internet access and the "Hardware of Their Dreams" package, with lifelong upgrades! Promotions, like all forms of advertising, must be written—and spoken—in your prospects' language.

Incorporate a Bit of Fantasy

We said *magic* before. Promotion takes that listener, viewer, or reader one step closer to your product, and tantalizes them. It dangles something in front of them that they really want. Notice I said something they *want*—not something they need.

"Hurry, Hurry, Hurry!"

"Step right up to the greatest store on earth; we've got everything you've ever wanted—strange, curious objects you've never even seen before! Be among the first to witness these oddities—and maybe even *own* them!"

The carnival barkers of old had it right. They embodied the essence of the art of promotion. They just didn't have the right product. You do. Combine a little of their showmanship with your integrity, and you'll win at promotion.

Phrases like "Enter as often as you wish" have become part of our vocabulary over the years. Promotion asks the consumer to take a chance on *you* and your business. Promotion gives the consumer a reason to try you out, to come to you—to step inside and take a look, when they might not otherwise have done so.

This book is full of examples of small businesses that were willing to take a chance to attract new customers. Are you? We'll take a look at some more of them, shortly.

TOOLBOX

If you advertise a promotion with the wrong incentives, your ad campaign will fail. Survey your customers, or a similar group of people, to determine what would really entice them to sample your business. This will help you avoid wasting media dollars.

WHAT GOES UP, MUST COME DOWN

There's a downside to promotion: If you promote too often, people will hold back, and may not buy from you because they're waiting for the next promotion. You've conditioned them to do just that.

Another danger to promotions is that they encourage price-conscious consumers to cherry-pick offers—bouncing from one company to another. This can absolutely destroy any shred of consumer brand loyalty that remains. Ron Ryan, a former vice-president of sales and marketing for Allied Old English, makers of Sorrell Ridge spreadable fruit, concurs.

"We were one of three brands that shared nearly equally in sales for this product category," he recalled. "Any time we promoted, we had to give away product—buy two flavors, and get the third. People would switch just to get the offer, then go back to the competing brand."

Promotion that depends on off-price selling or heavy couponing can also erode your price structure. When consumers become accustomed to paying the reduced price, they begin to *perceive the regular price as high.*

When it comes to promotional offers geared to attracting new customers, you run the risk of alienating your existing customers. They may be asking themselves why you're offering savings or incentives to "them" (those new customers). For example, I questioned my home heating oil contractor why there was no reward for my twenty years of customer loyalty to their company. The answer: "They don't do that in our business. Maybe they should, but they don't. They only make offers to new customers." That's nearly enough to send me looking for another company, where *I'll* be the new customer. It certainly doesn't encourage customers to stay in your camp.

TOOLBOX

Consider building promotions that encourage new customers as well as help to retain old ones. Reward customer loyalty and longevity.

Businesses with a high "churn" rate, like the cellular phone industry, experience the same problem. Wireless carriers are constantly offering promotions to attract new customers. The industry's answer to reducing the high customer turnover has largely been limited to locking customers into long-term contracts. However, when you, as a consumer, are midway through your contract and see more attractive incentives offered to new customers, it only makes you want to switch to a competing carrier. Ouch! It hurts when you shoot yourself in the foot. Are *you* promoting "upstream"?

TURKEYS DON'T FLY, AND SHUT-INS DON'T GO OUT

As you know by now, it is my mission with this book to tell you ways to screw up your advertising, so I'll do that again. As always, I promise to tell you how to fix it.

Do you remember the TV series *WKRP in Cincinnati*? It seems a certain radio station wanted to do a Thanksgiving promotion that involved dropping turkeys out of an airplane. And they found out, the hard way, that turkeys don't fly.

Does this stuff really happen? Yes. At the first radio station I worked for, we were in a turnaround situation. We finally pulled things together enough to get some nice prizes and do a promotion. As luck would have it, I had the chance to watch the morning deejay, as he was ready to notify the winner. Thank God it was *taped*, and not live. It went like this:

"Hello, is this Gladys Saunders of Ewing Township?"
"Yes."
"Do you know who this is?"
"No."
"This is Bill Jeffries of 920 TTM. Gladys, do you know why I'm
    calling you?"
"No."
"Well, I'm calling to tell you that you just won an all expenses paid
    trip to—Gladys? Are you there? Well, uh, isn't that great?
"No. My doctor says I can't go out."
"Well, you could give it to your daughter . . . "

Stuff happens. Most of it we can control, but not all of it. Try to goof-proof your promotions against embarrassment. Make them watertight, with contingencies. Remember, the unexpected is sure to happen.

ONWARD AND UPWARD

So, why bother? We need to promote for the same reason we cited earlier, when we said that everyone needs to continue to advertise. We need to promote because we all need to replace that part of our customer base that we lose—often through no fault of our own. We need to take out just a little more insurance, if you will, on getting that result. Promotion helps to increase the traffic count—whether it's walk-in, phone-in, mail-in, click-through, fly-in, or crash-in.

Okay, so I'll promote. But *when* should I promote? When will it help me the most and hurt me the least? Once again, *promote when there's less to lose.* Promote when you have a new product, service, or establishment. At that point in time, you have the lowest market share, so you only stand to *gain.*

Here's the perfect example: One of my clients opened a stand-alone carpet store. Like the doughnut shop we mentioned earlier, he has bought the first franchise in his region. Therefore, the store has no name recognition to coat-tail. He has to build it from scratch. He buys his product at extremely attractive wholesale prices and sells it to the public for equally attractive retail prices—in fact, truly unbeatable prices.

Although the store stands on a highway with adequate signage, it does not have exceptionally high visibility. Furthermore, he does not have a huge ad budget with which to drive traffic to the store. However, when people do set foot inside, they almost always buy something. This business is a prime candidate for promotion, because the store simply needs to overcome its name and location handicaps. With his unusually high closing ratio, as long as he raises his traffic count, his sales will increase. And that's why it makes sense for him to hold a drawing for a carpet giveaway. It doesn't cost him that much, but it has a high perceived value to the public.

Whatever you do, make sure your promotion conforms to all laws and regulations. (See Chapter 16, on advertising law, for more details.)

The phrase "void where prohibited by law" is an all-too-familiar part of our lexicon.

How to Really Promote Big by Playing the Odds

What other kinds of promotion can you do, besides those that offer price reductions? Let's talk about some of the ones that have proven successful, and have been tested, tried and true.

We'll start with a company in Reno, Nevada, called Hole in One International. From Hole in One, you can get anything from a scratch-off card game, to a golf promotion offering a prize for a hole-in-one, to a "guess how many balls are in the car," or "how many candies are in the jar" game. Hole in One's clients offer big, attractive prizes that get people excited and motivated to enter their contests. How do they do it?

Hole in One does it with an insurance policy that calculates the risk. In addition to paying for the advertising, you pay a percentage of the value of the prize, based on the odds of winning. Zack Woodhead of Hole in One tells me the amount of the insurance policy is often based on the history of his experience with such contests—how often anyone has won the prize with similar promotions.

I checked Hole in One's references, and found that they do indeed deliver on their promises. Charlie Santarelli has been running a golf tournament for a charity benefit in the Jamaica, New York, area for four years. When someone shot a hole-in-one, the company paid off—to the tune of *$1 million*! Not bad for $100 of insurance. Bob Weis of Legend Automotive in Columbia, Missouri, was able to give away a $40,000 Mercedes-Benz as a prize by insuring it with Hole in One International. Those are pretty good odds to come up with something that sounds that enticing to your customers. Check Hole in One's Web site at *www.hioi.com* and its sister company at *www.oddsonpromotions.com*.

STUNT MAN

You don't have to be in the movies to have one—or to be one. Former Philadelphia-area radio disc jockey Bo Weaver made headlines all the way to Sacramento, California, when he nailed himself inside the control room of 1,000-watt WTTM AM in Trenton, New Jersey. It was 1979; we were in the midst of the Arab oil embargo; people were frustrated over rapidly increasing gasoline prices.

Weaver announced that he had nailed himself in the studio in protest, and would not come out until the governor got on the phone with a solution to the gasoline crisis. To add icing to the cake, Weaver played a country-western protest song about the gasoline crisis—non-stop, for hours.

This went on from the afternoon to well into the night. Not only did Weaver jam his own station's switchboard—and the lobby—but the much bigger 50,000-watt rival station across town was bombarded with calls about Weaver's stunt. Even Larry King interviewed him at one point.

The moral of the story: It's not the power of the media, it's the power you *give* the media. Imagine if *your* business was there when it happened. Station sponsors didn't even mind that he skipped their commercials; they called in their support—just in case he got fired.

Once again, you can make *any* medium perform—if you know how, and if you give the people what they want. Bo Weaver did.

The Seven Commandments of Promotion

All right, all right; I'm still writing them. (Does everything have to be in tens?) So, what am I saying here? In order for a promotion not involving off-pricing to succeed, it needs several elements, including:

1. Thou shalt create a sense of urgency.
2. Thou shalt offer a highly motivating prize or incentive.
3. Thou must create a belief that the prize is winnable.

4. Thou shalt have a promotion with a natural tie-in to thy business.
5. Thou shalt create a promotion with a strong appeal to prospects that fit thy customer profile.
6. Thou must provide ease of entry or access to the promotion.
7. Thou shalt back the promotion with high-profile advertising to get the word out.

Yes, these *are* written in stone. Leave any of these out, and you risk weakening the results. Let's discuss each of these.

Thou Shalt Create a Sense of Urgency

If people feel there is no urgency to checking out your promotion now, they'll put it off—until it's over. However, you need to give them a reasonable time limit to visit, or to enter your contest. *Emphasize the deadline in all your advertising.*

Remember, people are jaded today. They've seen it all. They don't respond to "come in and get a free gift." How many key chains can you use? (I use them for luggage tags, myself.) Incentives must have a high perceived value, or people will not respond. (Note: That doesn't mean they have to cost *you* a lot. As long as the consumer would have to pay a lot, it has value to him or her.)

If your promotion involves off-price savings, *avoid using percentage discounts.* They don't accurately communicate the value of what you're offering. Instead, *use real dollar value savings.*

If it's a contest you're doing, make sure the prizes are worth coming in for. Once again, they may not cost *you* that much, but they must have value to your customers and prospects, or they will not bother to enter. (This is one of the chief causes of failure; it wasn't the advertising media that failed to perform; often, it was the *offer* that failed to excite the audience.)

Under Your Nose

I've always been amazed at how many businesses will look elsewhere for prizes. Very often, your own merchandise has great appeal to your prospects. If you're going to give something away, consider giving *that* away. It makes for a much stronger promotion to reinforce your own product. Why offer a Florida vacation when you sell beautiful clothes that your customers would love to own, or a car they long to drive?

If you create a theme for your promotion, it should also relate to your business. It's easier for customers to *remember to enter* that way. For example, if you rent party equipment—outdoor furniture, lanterns, grills, etc.—create a luau event. Hold an in-store party; serve food cooked on one of your grills, food kept heated in your chafing dishes, drinks served from your bar. Then, hold a drawing for a complete party, catered at the winner's home or office. *(Calculate the value of impressing each of the winner's guests!)*

I had a client who sold wicker, rattan, and bamboo furniture. People misperceived the product as just some flimsy porch furniture. We needed to demonstrate that you could actually furnish your entire house—living room, dining room, and bedroom—with this highly durable material.

Here's what we did. The store hired a disc jockey to spin records, and we held a wine and cheese party right in the store. Then, we invited customers to join the party, with our advertising. People got to really experience the furniture by actually sitting at a rattan bar, or at a glass-topped rattan table, or on a couch, while sipping their wine. On a Thursday night, when the rest of the shopping center was dead, we filled the store. The owners held prize drawings (for items that had sat in their stock room) and sold some merchandise.

Early in my advertising career, I met a man with two high-performance auto accessory shops—the kind of stores that sell chrome and customizing doodads for hot rod and racing enthusiasts. Hal Dunn decided to move one of the two stores right across the street, to a much larger location. He took over the former piano shop's warehouse behind the new store and converted it to a garage, adding turbocharging services as well.

Then came the big day. After selling his exotic Pantera and hocking everything he owned to buy the building and stock the place, it was time for a grand opening. But the piggy bank was broken. Advertise? "With what?" his partner asked.

Now, neither "Big H" nor I were prepared to give up. A few days and a lot of phone calls later, Hal had pulled whatever strings he needed to. The message hit the airwaves on three local radio stations, a local group of car restoration buffs known as "The Philadelphia Modifiers" set up a display of custom cars, and trash barrels full of ice and soda stood ready. Red, white, and blue banners beckoned the public. Neighboring businesses only wanted to know how he attracted more traffic to that corner than they had seen in over ten years.

Who can do this? Really, anyone can. Jerry Harmen has operated his Madison, New Jersey, camera shop for years. Surrounded by both malls and highway chain stores, and not a big advertiser, he has still managed to find a way to succeed—well enough to buy a second store in the nearby well-to-do town of Summit.

One year, for one week, Jerry hit up each of his vendors and created an in-store anniversary event. Not only did the vendors come up with advertising dollars for the event, and merchandise to give away as prizes, but they even sent their own people to conduct product demonstrations and answer questions. The phone rang, the doorbell rang—and the cash register rang.

What are *you* waiting for? Promote, promote, promote—and when you're done, promote some more!

On Your Mark, Get Set . . .

We've all heard the question, "If a tree falls in the forest and no one hears it, does it still make a sound?" Well, the same applies to promotion. Without proper advertising support, you can't hope to get people to enter your contest or take advantage of the savings you're offering. On the other hand, if you take the time to assemble a really winning promotion and you advertise it well, you stand to get far more response out of the advertising media than you would otherwise get. Remember my 856 restaurant patrons in one week? Or the 187 cars sold in five days? You can do it, too! Just support your promotion with enough well-planned advertising. Don't leave the engine out of your promotion.

TOOLBOX

Promote with media that will deliver and attract a new and different customer profile than your existing one.

Below-the-Belt Promotion

Most importantly, people have to believe that your promotion is real and legitimate. If it appears questionable in any way (e.g., that the odds of winning are too small, the prize isn't valued at what you say it is, it's too difficult to enter), forget it, because you can be sure your customers will. *Anything less than straightforward and above-board promotion will come back and hurt you*—even if it's technically legal.

This applies to discounting as well. When you issue coupons or honor offers that are "only good on Mondays and Tuesdays between the hours of 3 and 5 P.M., and only on this one rack of merchandise, and only after the first $50 purchased," forget it. *Make the promotion too restrictive, and no one will respond.* Worse yet, they'll shop with you, but they won't buy, and they surely won't return. Take a good, hard look at your offers. Are you doing this?

WORKS FOR THE LITTLE GUY

Don't think for a minute that promotion only works for companies like McDonald's. This book is full of small businesses that have promoted themselves successfully. Want to hear more? Okay, you win; here's more.

I had a client with a small chain of record shops. It was right at the time cassettes were just coming into vogue. We needed to get people to let go of their eight-tracks. If they embraced cassettes, installed cassette players in their cars, and bought home stereos with cassette players, then they would have to replace their favorite titles with cassettes. We ran a campaign inviting customers to trade in their eight-tracks and get credit toward new cassettes. We filled a trash barrel with eight-tracks in each store.

TOOLBOX

Devise promotions that play up attributes your competitors don't have . . . invite customers to bake the biggest cake, build the biggest sandwich, etc.

Meanwhile, suppose your margins are so thin that you can't discount your products heavily. Suppose you don't want to do contesting because you really only want serious prospective buyers, not just bodies in the door. Can you still promote? Yes, yes, yes!

Today, event-oriented promotions really can work, especially if your business caters to a leisure class of upscale consumers with some time on their hands. Here are just a couple of examples I've actually helped small retailers to create.

Several years ago, the Grumbacher Art Supply Company linked up with a West Coast art educator named Sue Scheewe. Together, they offered art supply stores an in-store seminar known as the "Paint It and Take It Workshop." Each participating store would schedule a workshop and advertise the event locally. It promised consumers, "Even if you never painted a picture before in your life, you will walk out with a finished painting in about two hours."

My client, Parsippany, New Jersey–based Du Pont Graphic Arts, offered it. People registered, and, as promised, they did indeed walk out with a finished painting inside of two hours—and they walked out with Grumbacher paint sets, too. Most of the registrants were either pregnant women or young mothers. The promotion worked like a charm. Check your industry's trade magazine, trade shows, and Web sites for similar prepackaged event promotions. Or, create your own. We did.

Taking a cue from the success of Du Pont's "painting for fun" promotion, I found another opportunity to create a similar event. Denville, New Jersey, retailer Richard Yobs runs a paint and decorating store called Painten' Place. (Yes, he's the guy who stood on his head for the newspaper ad.) Rich has always been receptive to ideas that make sense.

When I asked Rich what products he wanted to get behind, he mentioned Benjamin Moore's Wall Glazing Paint. "Wall what?" I asked. Wall glazing paint, I learned, is used to create special effects, like the popular faux finishes, such as painting your wooden mantelpiece to look like marble.

We asked local interior decorator June Fette to demonstrate these techniques at Painten' Place. Along with using local newspaper advertising, we submitted an article with a photo of June at work in her studio. Local papers ran the story, giving the workshop legitimacy and credibility as an educational event.

The result? We had to set up a *second* date to handle the overflow of response. Veni, Vidi, Visa—they came, they saw, they charged! Seeing is believing, and many of the participants bought the product demonstrated. Once again, without any giveaways or heavy discounting, we filled a store full of people seriously interested in buying. Yes, you can. *Do* try this at home!

Testing, One, Two, Three . . .

Remember when we talked about those products that are high-ticket, infrequent purchases—like carpeting? We mentioned the "once in ten years" purchasing cycle. Well, here's how to attack that problem. Set up a series of in-store decorating seminars. Invite local decorators to run them in your store. If they're sharp, they'll do it without asking for anything up front, in exchange for the chance to attract new clients. Now, approach your suppliers for vendor support funds. Next, tap any available co-op dollars you've earned. Finally, you and your ad counselors assemble a dynamite advertising campaign to invite the public.

What will you demonstrate? Everything from the seasonal color theory that tells people to select colors for their living environment that are compatible with their skin and hair tones, to do-it-yourself installation techniques, to how to coordinate ceramic tile with wood, carpet, and area rugs. Did we mention telling them how to co-ordinate their floor covering with wall coverings and furniture? You get the idea, now take it and run with it!

So, how does this apply to me, you ask? You're in the service business. Believe me, we *all* are. The trick here is to *adapt* what we tell you to *your* business, whether it's a better way to discount, a traffic-building giveaway, an in-store event, or a cause-related promotion.

Hey, you mean I can save the whales, offer a whale of a deal, give away a fishing trip, and teach people how to catch more fish, all at the same time? Well . . . maybe.

TOOLBOX

Each promotion should have one clear objective—to drive traffic, to move merchandise, to draw attention to a new location, to flatten a feisty competitor.

Can't I Just Tag Along?

The answer is yes. Attach yourself to other people's existing promotions. Sometimes you don't need to create your own promotion to succeed. In many industries with well-advertised national brands, manufacturers encourage local outlets to join in on their promotions. When you do, your advertising doesn't have to work as hard.

If you're a Chevrolet dealer, for example, and Chevy is offering consumers a chance to "See the U.S.A. in a Chevrolet," all you need to do is advertise that they can register to win that trip in *your* showroom. When they see and hear your ads, they'll remember all the national and regional advertising for the promotion. The advantage to you? You're coat-tailing all that national advertising for a small cost, and driving the local traffic to *your* business.

Look to see what national promotions *your* suppliers are doing. Tie in to them whenever possible. It gives your advertising both impact and momentum. Besides, you may not have to pay for those attractive prizes!

ALWAYS A WAY

"But I don't sell a nationally branded item backed by high-profile advertising," you say. You have to do it yourself, but you still need that extra sizzle and spice that promotion offers. How can you get it, if your resources are limited? Put your ears on, and your antennae up, 'cause I'm going to tell you.

You and your ad counselors should check with your local media. Unless you live in East Podunk, media outlets are always cooking up great promotions. Years ago, because radio got fewer ad dollars, local stations found it necessary to promote often. Now, with increasing competition for ad dollars, newspapers and local broadcast television stations have also jumped into the promotional game. Even coupon mailing companies are assembling promotions.

Very simply, media outlets offer lots of great ready-made promotions. You don't have to think them up; you don't have to put all the pieces together. Often, all you have to do is spend a certain amount of ad dollars (which you planned to do anyway), and you're in. So, what's in it for you?

Very often, media promotions are designed to drive traffic. They will involve some sort of in-store registration. That gives you an extra push. Often, they will also involve significant extra exposure—promotional mentions over and above your regular ads. Here again, you also benefit from the strength of all the participating advertisers. To top it off, in many cases, you don't have to put up the prizes. (However, when you do, you can usually barter the prizes for *more* ad space or time. This is the *one* time it makes sense to barter!) Let's look at just a few of these.

Bumper stickers. Radio stations want consumers to put stickers on their cars, so they encourage them to pick one up at sponsor locations. You get the extra mentions as a sponsor. Usually, listeners have a chance to win a prize by calling in when they hear their license plate announced, if their sticker was spotted. If they picked up the sticker at your business, that creates good-will. Furthermore, perhaps they win a prize from your establishment (or one of your dealers, if you're the supplier). When they come down to claim it, they see your merchandise. You can be sure they'll tell their friends and family about it. Every time they *use* their prize, they are reminded of your business. *Added bonus: While they're listening for their license plate to be announced, they'll hear your commercial!* You may find similar promotions offered by newspapers or TV stations, as well.

Lottery tickets. Some media outlets offer a secondary drawing for holders of losing lottery numbers, offering their own cash prizes. If you're a lottery agent, approach them with the idea of becoming a sponsor if it doesn't violate your agency agreement.

Treasure hunt. We had a phenomenal success with one of these, for ten years running, at a rock radio station. Listeners were told to visit sponsors who were announced daily. Sponsors were sent clues that were posted at their locations daily. The clues were repeated on-air. Each cryptic clue would help the listener figure out the location of the treasure. (It was always in a public place, in plain sight, visible from the right angle.) Each day, until someone found the treasure and turned it in, its value increased. At the conclusion, the station held a party for both the winner and the sponsors.

Cash-call jackpot. Because much of radio is still live, it lends itself well to this type of promotion. In its simplest form, a station announces an amount of money, invites listeners to call in, be the designated caller, and name the amount in the jackpot to win it. Each time they *don't* get a winner, they add money to the jackpot. My father used to call my mother three times a day from work, to make sure she knew the amount of the jackpot on his favorite station. Once again, the listener loyalty and attention that results means more attention paid to your ads, as well. (Yes, bribery works!) Here's the spin you, as a sponsor, can put on this one: Ask the station to require listeners to register in-store, fax in, mail in, or e-mail in, in order to enter. Rather than opening the phones to the public, the station can announce that only preregistered listeners can play. If you're a retailer, you get foot traffic. If not, you as a sponsor can still benefit by having your name on the printed entry blanks or the station's registration area of the Web page. Always a way!

Name that tune, or secret sounds. This is a popular, tried and true one that never goes out of style. The radio deejay on the air plays brief clips of either familiar songs or of sound effects, and invites his or her audience to call in and try to guess what they heard. Sponsor it, and you'll get the audience's ears when it is *paying very close attention.*

WXYZ discount cards. This is a common variation on the bumper sticker. Stations register listeners at live broadcasts, fairs, nightclub appearances, and other large-crowd events. Listeners get a free plastic card with a list of discounts and special cardholder offers. Often, cards are numbered, with periodic on-air announcements of winning numbers. I worked for one station that added extra hoopla when they registered their one-hundred-thousandth cardholder.

Stations like KLIF in Dallas, Texas, have well-oiled promotional machines. They capture data on cardholders and their interests. Periodically, they will mail or e-mail cardholders with special offers for travel deals and other opportunities offered by sponsors. (Listeners have already indicated their interest in these items, making them highly qualified prospects.) This is good value-added, multimedia promotion for the advertiser as well.

These "affinity cards" help make your advertising tangible. When you see listeners flash that card, you know your advertising is working. (It is, in essence, a "radio coupon.") A word of caution: Three things determine how successful these card programs will perform:

Offers. How attractive your offer and the other advertisers' offers are. If the offers are chintzy, people will not even bother to carry or use the card. (At one radio station where I worked, we required a certain minimum offer.)

Circulation. How many cards are in circulation at the time you advertise the offer. (Ask! It makes a big difference.) Look for at least 10,000; more, if you're in a large city.

Exposure. How well both you and the media promote the card and its offers. (You should cross-promote it in your other advertising, as well.) If they really get behind the card with prizes, with constant on-air mentions, and with off-air promotion as well, the card program can truly produce results for the sponsors.

The above are just a brief sampling of the existing media promotions you can tie into. There are tons more. You and your ad counsel should be alert to special events. Very often, when the media hold their events, they will have special sponsorable promotions as well. In some cases, if you approach them, they will entertain adding your promotion onto the event.

When I worked for WOR/New York, then the largest talk radio station in America, they were celebrating their seventy-fifth anniversary. The station held the event at the Rutgers University Athletic Center. Because they are a heritage station broadcasting a family-oriented talk format for three generations, they cater to the older population.

The media refer to these types of opportunities as NTR ("nontraditional revenue"). For them, it means generating income in ways besides selling ad space or air time. For you, it means *more selling opportunities,* especially face-to-face with new prospects. At WOR, like many of the more sophisticated operations, sponsors of the station's special events are often given a mailing list of preregistered attendees after the event, allowing them to conduct follow-up marketing.

I worked with one of the longest continuous advertisers on the station. The Flemington Fur Company in Flemington, New Jersey, had built its business on the station for over forty years. When they heard about the anniversary celebration, they offered to give away a $10,000 ranch mink coat. I saw a tearfully happy listener take it home. Your warm and fuzzy opportunity is waiting!

Very often, because the media *are* the media, they get press on practically everything they do. With many of the ownership restrictions lifted, media companies are now able to own multiple properties in the same marketplace. This allows them to engage in more self-promotion and more cross-promotion as well. What's in it for you?

Well, many of the media's promotions get press coverage. If you're a part of them, you may stand to get some extra press as well. Here's an example of larger-than-life promotion. After years of running a Halloween party for its listeners that grew from a restaurant to an ice skating rink to a shopping mall, New Jersey rock radio station WDHA-FM eventually blew the event up to a full-size sports arena concert/costume party, complete with big-name stars.

To put a little extra spin on it, I suggested they put the word out on the air and invite listeners to compete for the chance to have their wedding at the event. Think about it: The press and the TV cameras just love to pick up the unusual—and I'd call a costumed wedding with 10,000 guests in a sports arena more than slightly unusual. Imagine if *your* banner was hanging there!

TOOLBOX

Flamboyant, outrageous promotions will usually attract press coverage: Consider the best-dressed pet contest for your formal-wear business; the highest mileage klunker for your auto dealership; a body-painting contest for your cosmetics shop.

STILL MORE PROMOS

Had enough? Of course not! That's why I'm here; to satisfy your promotional appetite. So here are a few more; see if you can use any of these ideas for your business.

Passbook (or passport) to savings. This can work for any retailer, and may be adaptable to other types of businesses, as well. In your advertising (in all media), tell your customers they can pick up their passbook from you. Once they register, each time they make a purchase, they accrue "interest," or credit toward future merchandise. They must present the book and have it updated. For the customer, it works just like a bank account! For you, it's a loyalty builder, designed to encourage repeat purchases. At the same time, you also achieve data capture for a mailing list. Now you can advise these same customers of new merchandise, expansion, etc.

Trading days. Offer a trade-in allowance on an old VCR (working or not), against the purchase of a new DVD player—or a trade-in allowance on an old turntable toward the purchase of a new CD player.

Jingle and logo contest. Invite the public to compete for prizes; have them create an identity campaign for you, based on their impressions of your business. Publish and air the winning entries.

Why I love 1-800-GOOD STUFF. Yes, it's so simple, even *children* can do it! In your advertising, invite kids to write an essay on why they love your product, service, or establishment. Ask local child advocates to serve as judges—teachers, day-care workers, pediatric nurses, etc. Publish and air the winning kids with their entries.

Treasure chest. An oldie, but a goodie. Your advertising invites the public to come to your location(s) and try out the key they received in the mail. The one that opens the chest wins the prize certificate inside. Many variations on this one are possible.

Casino night. Check the legality of this one for your area. Many vending houses rent out gaming equipment. Turn your location into a casino. Everyone wins when you fill the house with potential customers!

Trash for cash. In your advertising, invite your customers to bring in their recyclables and get a dollar amount credited toward your merchandise. They can earn credit by the pound, or by the piece.

Game shows. Capitalize on the recent resurgence of their popularity. You can actually bring in a traveling game show, complete with a professional host and the whole stage set. For example, Barry Herman Entertainment of Livingston, New Jersey, has a sports trivia game—this works as a great fundraiser, too.

Pet costume contest. If Buffy can, Rover can. Do this one, and you're bound to draw a crowd, and maybe get some press coverage, too.

TOOLBOX

If you have hard-to-find, trendy, popular merchandise that engenders a cult-like following, create promotions that encourage your customers to advertise for you. (For example, a car customizing contest, awarding prizes for the most artistic paint job, best vintage restoration, etc.)

What else can you do? Thank you for asking. Hold a blood drive at your place of business, complete with phlebotomists (blood technicians) dressed as vampires (or, medieval characters with phony leeches!). Tie into any holidays that make sense for your business. Offer a little romance for Valentine's Day (win a getaway); save or win green for St. Patrick's Day, etc.

How about tying in to big events that people really want to attend? We ran a townwide promotion in Madison, New Jersey, which calls itself "The Rose City." Advertising invited the public from Madison and the surrounding communities to come to downtown merchants displaying a poster, to enter and win a trip to—you guessed it—the Rose Bowl! Why not?

Where There Are Cars . . .

A word about traffic: This story deserves to be told, and retold. I had a client who operated four fast-food fish and chips franchise restaurants. He noticed that one of his locations just seemed light on traffic. The restaurant was easily accessible, with plenty of pass-through traffic. When he surveyed his staff, he found that they lived in the immediate neighborhood and walked to work. Very simply, there were no cars in the parking lot at lunch hour. When people drove by and saw an empty lot, they just kept going.

The next week, the manager instructed every employee to bring a car to work, even if they lived right next door. They did, and as people drove by and saw a parking lot full of cars, they pulled in to join them. How's that for inexpensive promotion?

TOOLBOX

A restaurateur chose one night a month to randomly surprise his customers by picking up everyone's check. Nobody knew which night it would be . . . so they all kept showing up, again and again. (P.S.: It only cost him about 3 percent.) Promote with the element of surprise.

➡ The Really Big One

Here it is, the one you've all been waiting for—the granddaddy of all promotions. This is the one I always wanted to do and never had the chance to run. I humbly offer it up to you. This is not for the faint of heart. Ready? Here goes my recipe for the ultimate success story:

Take one new home builder, add one realtor; gently fold in several spicy home furnishings dealers and contractors. Run a generous advertising schedule. Invite listeners, readers, and viewers to pick up clues and comb the countryside. When the lucky (and skillful) person finds the right house, they'll discover the key that opens the door. Once inside, they'll find the instructions on how to claim the deed.

Think about the benefits to this one. The winner takes all (a new home for free!); the sponsors get some very noticeable press; the media promoting the contest builds huge circulation and ratings during the whole process. (If they're smart, they'll be reporting on the events as they progress.)

PROMOTING PROMOTING

How do I promote thee? Let me count the ways. Provided you are not cannibalizing your existing sales by offering unnecessary discounts to people already willing to pay your prices, promotion can fuel your growth. Just remember: Don't do it too often, don't alienate existing customers, keep it legitimate (both legal and ethical), keep it exciting and interesting, keep it relevant to your customers and prospects—and don't forget to follow up with your newfound prospects. If you turn the traffic you gained from promotion into regular, repeat customers, you'll come out ahead.

The Highlight Zone: "Resting on Laurels"

Submitted for your approval, a town with a thriving downtown business district. On either side of the street, you'll find every type of shop or office you could ever want to visit—from the barber to the shoemaker; from the haberdashery to the butcher.

The perfect place to do business? Perhaps. Or perhaps not. In a moment, you'll know the answer, here in the Highlight Zone.

Everything about Springfield looks inviting. The business owners are friendly, they keep their stores and offices clean and freshly painted, and they all use their local advertising media to remind the 25,000 residents to pick up that loaf of bread on the way home or to take advantage of the new riding mowers at McIntyre's Hardware.

There's only one problem in Springfield: The town is changing. For years, the only way in and out of town was Main Street. Now the highway department has begun work on a new bypass around the center of town. Human nature being what it is, that's just what people will do; bypass the Main Street business district.

Then, there's the mountain that always blocked radio and TV signals from the nearby big city. It's being blasted to make way for the highway, meaning that businesses in Springfield will have to compete with outside advertisers.

Enter Ted Wylie, advertising man and Springfield's newest resident. He likes to fight fire with fire. If conditions can change, so can the way Main Street Springfield promotes itself. If you take a closer look, you'll see Ted Wylie signing up all the businesses in Springfield for a group advertising promotion designed to keep residents shopping in town, with special discounts—one that also invites surrounding area residents to come visit Springfield. So you see, what goes out, must come in.

Look around your town. Perhaps there's a Ted Wylie about to move in. Welcome him in, to the Highlight Zone.

◀◀ Time Capsule: Eat at Albie's

This time we are going to use the way-back machine to check out a restaurant with a family connection—that of Einstein.

See how it attracts all the Princeton intelligentsia? First rule for a good promotion: Attract a qualified audience for your product. And check out the back of the menu: "Win a neutron burger; just bombard us with your name and address as often as you can."

And then there's the blackboard by the entrance: "Write your own formula; if our chefs like your recipe better than theirs, it goes on the menu, and you eat free." Now, *that's* how to get the best talent to work for you, and at the right price.

Here's my favorite one of all: "It's Friday. Gone fission; the first person to correctly guess the catch of the day gets to charge lunch to the house."

I hope that's a positive charge. I guess fish really is brain food, after all.

Albie's really got a good thing going here—a theme restaurant just for smart folks. And the promotions really make them want to keep coming back, and to keep telling more friends. ▶▶

chapter 16

Do's, Don'ts, Can'ts, Won'ts: Sobering Truths about Advertising Law

The motto for my alma mater, Kean University, which was founded as a teacher's college, reads: "Who Dares to Teach Must Never Cease to Learn." I like to learn. I prefer to learn from the masters. I suggest you do, as well.

Douglas Wood, a partner in the law firm of Reed Smith LLP (with offices in Los Angeles, New York City, Washington, D. C. and throughout the world) literally wrote the book on the subject of advertising law. Wood has practiced advertising law since 1977, and is the author of *Please Be Ad-Vised*, published by the Association of National Advertisers.

More than fifteen years ago, I attended one of Doug Wood's workshops, which was offered by my local ad club. Since then, I have referred to his materials whenever I had a question about anything related to advertising law. You may find the book a bit weighty. (It's about the size of a large metropolitan telephone directory.) However, I suggest you *refer your ad agency to it*.

Doug has made it much simpler these days. If you don't have time to wade through the book, or it's not convenient to attend one of his firm's seminars, you can get not only the most accurate, but the most up-to-date information, by subscribing to his firm's e-magazine, Adlaw by Request (*www.adlawbyrequest.com*). Doug and his firm are a living example of principled people who are giving back to their community. Yes, they've enjoyed prosperity—which they've earned—but *their* advertising has "grown a conscience."

In addition to information about the law firm, you'll find plenty of useful free information, including digests of relevant advertising case law—and *free forms that will save you a great deal of money and trouble.* What kind of trouble? Keep reading; we'll tell you. Make sure to direct your ad counselors to the Web site, as well.

Ad Police?

They exist! In an earlier chapter, I mentioned businesses I knew that received fines in the mail from their state's Consumer Affairs Departments—without warning, due process, or appeal, I might add.

We are in the era of the police state. Make no mistake about it. As of now, only your dreams are free from scrutiny. (Now, if we could just work out some sponsorships. . . .) Be absolutely clear that *every ad you put out in nearly every medium will go under the legal microscope.* So, how can you avoid criminal fines and civil suits when you prepare your advertising? We'll tell you how.

There are several critical areas of advertising law that you should at least have an awareness of. Your ad counselors should at least have a working knowledge of these. Here's a brief overview, taken from materials prepared by our expert, Doug Wood; we'll discuss each in a little bit more detail, afterward.

Highlights of Ad Law

Support for product claims. Without proper support, you leave your business open to "both private lawsuits and governmental intervention," in the words of Douglas J. Wood, Esquire.

Relationships with suppliers and advertising media. You and your agency must properly handle contracts and licenses for the use of all talent and materials. These should spell out both who is liable for payment, and who owns what.

Comparative advertising. You must portray both your products and your competitors' attributes fairly.

Product liability. If your advertising encouraged people to buy or use a product deemed unsafe, it will draw fire in the form of lawsuits. (Does your ad agency carry errors and omissions insurance? In fairness to them, perhaps they should, if this applies to you.)

Using names and likenesses. You must secure proper permission to use people's names, faces, and voices in your advertising— by the way, death does not always qualify as a release. (Your honor, in order to call our next witness, I request permission to hold a séance. . . .)

Copyrights, trademarks, and patents. Ideas are not protected; the *expression* of those ideas *is*. You may be able to protect your ad campaigns from a rip-off, but you must also exercise caution in using others' protected materials.

Testimonials. There is a whole set of rules. In a nutshell, the person must actually use the product, and the endorsement must not be misleading.

Demonstrations. Similar to testimonials, they must be true and genuine.

Sweepstakes and contests. If it contains three elements, it will constitute an illegal lottery. These are: A *prize* is offered; there is an element of *chance*; and the consumer has to give a *consideration*, or something of value.

Flags, money, and stamps. Our expert's advice: Avoid using flags; if you must reproduce money, do it only in black and white—and only more than 150 percent or less than 75 percent of its actual size. Use the same size guidelines for uncancelled U.S. stamps reproduced in color.

Words You Can't Say, or Maybe Shouldn't Say

Guarantee or warranty. You must specify where the consumer can get the full details (in-store, online, etc.). You see, George Carlin was right!

Free. Yes, you can say it, but be prepared to prominently describe any conditions or limitations on the offer.

Sale. As with *free*, you must disclose any conditions or limitations. You may not be able to call it a sale if you offer the item for that price too often.

New. Except in test markets for limited times in a designated area, you may only use the word if the product is genuinely new or significantly changed. Repackaging does *not* qualify as new.

So much for the eye-openers; let's get to the meat of the matter. We live in a complicated, regulated, and litigious society. You and your advertising counsel *must* factor that into every campaign you produce. It's simply *not* worth the cost to defend expensive claims against your business.

BEGGING, BORROWING, OR STEALING?

Doug Wood candidly described the dilemma of today's ad agencies this way:

"People expect the content of a campaign to be current and topical, and to conjure up things consumers are used to seeing, and sort of associated with something that's 'hot' in the marketplace today; whether it be music or film or a TV show. There's a natural inclination to ride on the coat-tails or trade off of something that's been created in other media. As a result, agencies are often drawing the line between borrowing and taking the intellectual property of others for advertising campaigns that are associated with other creative content. The dilemma for agencies is, when do they cross the line between fair use—taking ideas, which are not protected—as opposed to the actual expression, in movies or TV, or books?"

Let's take a practical example. Suppose the new *Star Wars* movie has come out, and I run a small business trading in northern California. I decide I want to have a *Return of the Jedi* sale and compare my product to Light Sabers, saying, "It works just as fast as a Light Saber," or "It cuts as well as a Light Saber." What have I opened up here?

According to Doug Wood, here's the situation:

"Clearly, the idea of a space adventure is open to anybody to create one of their own, and no one can have a monopoly on that, whether it's *Star Wars*, *Star Trek*, or *Invasion of the Body Snatchers*. What *is* protectable is the original expression that a particular producer brings to that idea. In the case of *Star Wars*, the idea of a Light Saber is unique to *Star Wars*."

Wood goes on to define our hypothetical infringement, as follows:

"When you take the next step and use actual indicia, that's when you cross the line. George Lucas and Lucasfilm would, you can be assured, take umbrage and come after somebody for that. And rightfully so, because those concepts in the movie are actively licensed, and are truly valuable works. The law would say that just because you think it's funny, creative, or would help you sell your product, you cannot take out of the stream of commerce things created by the original producers that would create revenue."

TOOLBOX

Both your own creations (intellectual property) and someone else's are protected, as long as they have commercial value. Respect others' creations as you would have yours respected.

DEFENSE

Let's look at the flip side of the situation. Suppose you, as a small-business owner, have created the protectable property. How can you protect your product or process from either another small, or even an extremely large, business ripping it off? In fact, Congress is mandated by the U.S. Constitution to pass laws concerning copyrights and patents. Doug Wood describes them as "constitutionally permitted monopolies."

There are four ways to protect what you have created—including your ad campaign. Check to see which of these may apply. Doug Wood defines them for us, as follows:

Patent. If you have a particular product or process that is unique or novel and has never been used before, and you can get a patent on it, that is the broadest and the *best protection* you can get for something. It is costly, however.

Copyright. Copyright protects the manner in which you *express* your ideas. Your company produces a new product and advertises it; the words and the visuals are protectable. If you have a design feature not related to the operation of the product, that is also protectable by copyright, as a piece of art. (The bubble-like shape of your portable radio, for example.) Wood advises that today, *U.S. law protects your works from the moment you create them. You don't have to file anything* anywhere; you don't have to put notice on anything. You used to have to register works; that's no longer the case. (My advice, however; you should consider placing a copyright notice on your work to deter a would-be rip-off; also, registering the work will help support your claim that you authored the work first, in the event of an infringement.)

Trademarks. Trademarks are words, logos, symbols, or slogans that indicate the source or origin of the product. After doing the appropriate searches, you file with the U.S. Patent and Trademark Office. The process takes anywhere from six months to a year and a half. Of particular interest to small businesses is the fact that the law changed a few years ago. Now you can get "intent to use" protection. Previously, if you invested in developing a product, but somebody beat you to the marketplace, you were out of luck. Our expert advises that companies developing new products file this application well before they begin trading.

Trade secrets. An example: the "nooks and crannies" in Thomas's English Muffins. How do they do that? It is a closely guarded secret, known by only a few. Thomas's successfully challenged former executives who left the company and attempted to create a product with similar attributes. These are difficult to protect; it must be a mystery that someone can't simply figure out by looking at the product, or by "reverse engineering" the product.

WANDERING GENERALITIES

What happens when a product becomes a generic? Does it lose its protectability with the above devices? How do you prevent this from happening?

Doug Wood points to Xerox and Kleenex. These products captured and dominated the landscape in their product categories so well that people referred to competitors by *their* brand names. How did they manage to maintain their trademark protection and not become generics? True to form, let's look at the screwups first.

Doug Wood points out that these two did *not* behave like Thermos, who lost their trademark. Thermos's main competitor, Aladdin, started calling their hot and cold fluid containers "thermos," using the word as a noun. The kicker: "Thermos themselves used the term in their advertising and marketing as a *noun* instead of an adjective. Linoleum, aspirin, escalator, and nylon were all once trademarks that have been lost, because they've been used improperly in the marketplace. In the minds of consumers, they become the generic noun, as opposed to an adjective. Technically, *a trademark is always an adjective that describes the generic noun.* It is always Kleenex tissue, Sanka decaffeinated coffee, Xerox photocopies, etc."

What's the exception? "Have you driven a Ford lately?" is technically an incorrect usage, but the Ford Motor Company doesn't expect anyone else to start calling their cars "Fords."

When the public misuses your company's marks, you need to be concerned.

Just Kidding

What about satire? What is it, when can you use it, does it infringe on someone else—and is it *itself* protectable?

If you're merely trading off on someone else's goodwill, you're going to have problems. However, there is a notion of satire or parody accepted in intellectual property law as a legitimate expression. Doug Wood remarks, "Just because it's funny doesn't mean it's satire. Satire means you are poking fun or ridiculing the original work."

He gives the example of the cast of *Saturday Night Live* performing the song "I Love Sodom," as a parody of the song "I Love New York." By making the statement that New York is like Sodom, the work is more than just a borrowing of elements from the original song, placed in a funny situation. To quote Wood, "Advertisers stumble when they fail to understand the concept of parody and satire. Very rarely will advertising be created that has the intent of ridiculing something. If you talk to an advertising professional, they'll tell you that you're not going to sell a lot of product by ridiculing an icon."

Has it ever been done successfully? Yes. Coors did an ad with actor Leslie Nielsen dressed like the Energizer bunny going across the screen. The court overruled the lawsuit challenging the campaign, holding it to be a legitimate parody. Of course they did—we all know the difference between a silver bullet and a copper top, don't we?

If It Looks Like a Duck and Sounds Like a Duck, Shoot It

The use of look-alikes and sound-alikes in advertising presents some real problems. When Lincoln-Mercury first introduced the Sable, they wanted to use Bette Midler's song, "Do You Want to Dance?" They approached her; her agent said she doesn't do commercials, so they went to one of her backup singers and asked her if she could sound like Bette Midler. The singer agreed, and the company intentionally produced a commercial with her sounding like Bette Midler singing her signature song. Ms. Midler, of course, sued—and won.

But a few years earlier, Goodyear Tire and Rubber had attempted to do the same thing with Nancy Sinatra's song, "These Boots Are Made for Walking." The California court had ruled that there was no protection for the way somebody sounds.

What was the difference? According to Doug Wood, "The court simply did not want to face as big an icon as Bette Midler with the position that there was no protection for the way she sounds. So, they created a new tort in California that said if you use the sound of a famous individual for the purposes of earning a profit, you can be sued." (Author's note: The reality is, except where states have instituted frivolous lawsuit statutes, you can *always* be sued. That *doesn't* mean the plaintiff will always prevail.)

Singer Tom Waits sued Frito-Lay, winning over $1 million for a similar occurrence, soon afterward. In fact, Wood points out, the awards got larger as time went on. Consider this: All of these would-be rip-off artists probably could have hired the best talent to create a fresh, original campaign for far less than the settlements they wound up paying—not to mention the cost of the negative press that resulted.

What about impersonations? Can you use one, followed by a disclaimer? Answer: Only if you're able to "slip below the radar."

Doug Wood relates that you may hear these on radio, simply because it's often local, and people get away with it. You wouldn't be likely to see one of these on national television, for example. Wood related that using a disclaimer may actually be worse, because it shows an *intent*. This could result in greater damages than simple negligence.

TOOLBOX

Remember, in news reporting, the principal of fair comment applies. Public figures have fewer rights to privacy than private persons. However, this does *not* apply to advertising. If the communication is designed to make money, you can't trade on someone's fame without his or her permission.

Wanted, Dead or Alive

Can you use someone's name, likeness, or voice if they're dead? Answer: Only if you lived in Tennessee when "The King" died. (We're referring to Elvis. We're assuming he *is* dead.)

The court initially held that Elvis had become public domain. So the Tennessee legislature quickly passed a law to protect his legacy. This began an entire trend to protect the likenesses of celebrities after death.

Many states have similar laws, with Indiana's being the most noteworthy. In that state, for *100 years* after death, it is illegal to use the person's name, likeness, or "indicia of identity." ("Indicia" is a vague concept, and could refer to something as innocuous as a candelabra on a piano—signifying Liberace.)

Only in New York state does a deceased person have no rights of privacy or publicity. You can freely use his or her name or likeness in advertising there. But, "Very few campaigns published or broadcast in New York touch just New York," cautions Doug Wood. Most of these spill over into the neighboring states of New Jersey, Pennsylvania, and Connecticut, which all have laws protecting the rights of deceased celebrities.

In general, the right of privacy from publicity survives *fifty years* after death. Practically speaking, after that you will seldom encounter heirs to challenge you.

> **TOOLBOX**
>
> What's good for the advertising goose is not always good for the advertising gander. Laws related to infringement vary from state to state. Look before you honk.

AND THE WINNER IS . . .

In addition to the brief overview we gave you earlier in this chapter, here is some valuable, cogent advice from Doug Wood, for small businesses considering engaging in contest promotions:

Simple, random drawings are not prohibited in any state in the United States. If the prize value exceeds $5,000, you have to bond and register it in New York and Florida, a relatively simple process.

More complex contests, like those involving scratch-off games, collecting bottle caps to see what you've won, etc., have extremely complicated laws that differ from state to state. *Get qualified legal advice before you try this—at home, or anywhere else!* These are criminal, not civil laws; violate them, and you could serve jail time.

Insured contests are perfectly legitimate, as long as there is a reasonable possibility of winning the stated prize. The odds can be great, as long as they are not physically or practically impossible. Provided there is not a deception that misrepresents the prize as winnable, there is no problem.

It is extremely rare for the actual conduct of the promotion itself to be taken to task; it is almost always *the advertising that promotes the contest* that is called into question. The question is, what do the consumers exposed to the advertising perceive about the contest? What do they think they have to do in order to win, for example? (The hotly contested one in recent years has involved magazine subscription offers tied to sweepstakes.)

MAKES YOU IRRESISTIBLE

What kind of regulations govern product claims? What can you say about what your product does? Doug Wood cites that advertising executives often try to justify claims by leaving the realm of common sense. He advises the advertiser to "Ask yourself what you as a consumer would expect to get by using the product. If you don't come up with the same message you get in your advertising, chances are, your advertising is deceptive."

TOOLBOX

One constant principle of advertising law: You not only get what you pay for, you must also pay for what you get. Advertising media and supplier organizations track deadbeat clients—in short, the word gets around. If you stiff one company in the business, nearly everyone knows about it. Make honorable settlements; attempt to make reasonable adjustments if you didn't get what you paid for.

Once again, the amount of exposure you risk with the product claims you make relates directly to the level of media you advertise in. Chances are good that your matchbook ad will escape detection. However, our expert advises that as you progress up the line with higher profile media, you risk greater scrutiny. Regulators simply don't have the resources to police everything. Regulators have to focus on advertising that has the most effect on the consumer, like network television.

Doug Wood notes that, "The law is the same and the criteria are the same, but the risk is clearly different," when you advertise in bigger media outlets.

CYBERSPACE: "FREE ZONE"?

What about the Internet? It's still largely unregulated. Does that mean I can make any claims I want, in my online advertising? At this writing, the Federal Trade Commission (FTC) has issued statements indicating their intention to apply the same standards as they normally use to Internet advertising.

Doug Wood indicates that although the FTC has not shown signs of creating new regulations just for the Internet, they have already entered into agreements with foreign governments to jointly go after deceptive marketers. The general feeling of the current U.S. administration and Congress is to give the medium some time to grow. To date, e-commerce is being encouraged, somewhat unfettered, without taxation and over-regulation.

However, Europe and other parts of the world have not taken the same posture, notes Wood. Global marketers could be affected by this. If you have assets or sales in those countries, it could impact your business, if you trade online in a country that regulates Internet advertising. Blocking your site may not be technically feasible. However, they could seize your assets.

Could a global advertising medium like the Internet result in a flood of more knockoff products into the United States? The downloading of music or photos doesn't pose as much of a threat, because the record companies and the film companies have the means to fight the infringement. It's more of a problem for the small entrepreneur, notes Wood. Say you created a great new product and decided to launch it on the Internet. Are you more vulnerable to ripoffs? Yes.

The issue of protection for online marketers starts with this question: What does it cost to get to market? So-called "barriers to entry" often protect intellectual property. For example, it may not be costly to duplicate a tape, but it could be expensive to make an effective intrusion into the marketplace.

But the Internet breaks the barriers to entry down to near zero, according to Doug Wood. This gives the "entrepreneurial infringer" the opportunity to penetrate the market in a more meaningful way than ever before. If people do this from certain countries, you will have no intellectual property protection whatsoever.

Marketers beware: You may have to go to that country to sue the infringes, in order to stop them. This could prove costly. The result is that, ironically, we have created "barriers to protection." The originator of the product doesn't have the money to protect it, and the infringer can take advantage of the originator, almost with impunity.

The answer? *Build your base offline first.* Then, when you have the resources to protect your product, go global.

TOOLBOX

In spite of less regulation on the Internet, you are still responsible for your Web site content. Be sure your Web developers do not infringe on anyone else's material when building, maintaining, and populating your site.

Big Guy, Little Guy

In recent years, several cases have surfaced in which composers have challenged high-profile, famous, well-to-do musicians and accused them of plagiarizing their work. The courts have found merit and awarded the plaintiffs generous settlements.

So there is some measure of equal protection for creative works. Just how level is the playing field? Doug Wood tells us, "The standards of proof and the standards of liability are pretty much the same. The Internet has raised two copyright standards. The first is *access*—you can't copy something unless you've seen it. Secondly, you need *substantial similarity*.

"Historically, access has always been extremely difficult to prove," he explained. "It's hard for me to say 'I have proof that you read my book, heard my music; or, I've got a receipt that you bought it.' Usually, you prove infringement with works that are so similar it is impossible that you could have come up with it independently.

"The Internet poses an entirely different scenario," he continued. "In a recent case, Florida Citrus ran a TV commercial with a talking ham sandwich in the refrigerator. A California-based Internet newsletter ran a story about a ham sandwich that lived in the back of a Cadillac and fed information to try and rid the world of Communists.

"When the citrus campaign came out, that company sued Florida Citrus and the ad agency, the Richards Group in Dallas, Texas, for copyright infringement. A ham sandwich is a ham sandwich, but the interesting thing about this case is that the Internet company was able to show that the creative people from the ad agency logged onto their site, where they had the ham sandwich story, *before* they came up with the ham sandwich for Florida Citrus. Gotcha!

"So in this case, they could actually show *access*, which is a rarity. When you can show access, the bar of substantial similarity falls considerably. There's a natural thought process on the part of the judge or jury that if you *saw* it, you *must have* copied it. Therefore, the Internet may change copyright cases because we can prove access, unlike before," adds Doug Wood.

FORM FOLLOWS FUNCTION

Wood reiterates my concern for advertisers and agencies protecting themselves through contracts. He notes that small businesses in particular are "loath to use contracts." There is never an excuse in business not to have a contract between people who are dealing—even if it's nothing more than a simple letter signed by the two, agreeing on the essential terms and conditions. Failing to do that is just plain poor business—and the advertising agency business is notorious for not having contracts. Years ago, people would buy millions of dollars worth of media without any signed contract, and it worked.

TOOLBOX

Review media contracts carefully. If they read that you and your ad agency are jointly and severally liable, it means you could be held responsible for payment of ad space or time you already paid to your agency, if they went out of business and failed to pay the media.

"Largely, it still works for media. Where it doesn't work is for print suppliers, and between agencies and advertisers when things are falling out and they have problems." For that reason, he recommends the forms his firm has provided free on the Web site referenced earlier in this chapter.

What about issues of liability, when there are no clear contracts in place? Let's look at another hypothetical scenario: I have a small company; I hire your ad agency to handle my new product introduction. You, in turn, hire various subcontractors—a jingle writer, musicians, photographers, videographers, etc. Somebody accuses us of not only infringing on their product, but also infringing on their ad campaign, saying it's a knockoff. In the absence of having proper agreements among ourselves, we have issues of liability with respect to each of the individual subcontractors, as well as the agency and the advertiser.

"Absent a contract," Wood said, "as the advertiser, my position is going to be 'I hired you; you know advertising; you (the ad agency) were negligent at some point, and I'm going to look for you to pay the freight on what's happened here.' Of course, an agency will try to offload that on the supplier who created the problem. Chances are, those suppliers have far less money than the agency does. The outside complainer will go after the advertiser, who usually, in the string, has the most money. It becomes a huge mess over who's going to pay what.

"But if you have a contract that specifies liability, then there's not an issue. Cases then settle for a lot less, and are a lot less disruptive," he noted.

TOOLBOX

Make sure your agreements with ad agencies clearly spell out who owns what. *They* are responsible for doing the same with *their* subcontractors. Also, make sure to secure release forms whenever you hire talent (actors, announcers, models, singers, dancers) appearing in your ads. This grants you their permission to use their likeness or voice without additional compensation.

Meanwhile, "When you hire freelancers, they own any creative work they produce, because they're not employees," Wood pointed out. "Absent an agreement in writing that transfers ownership to you, signed by them, you don't own that work. Chances are, as far as your advertiser is concerned, they own what they pay you for. But, in reality, they don't, unless you've properly set up contracts signed by the supplier. Absent that, an agency can very often get caught in the middle."

As Wood points out, this can affect the continuing use of materials in a campaign. He has seen sloppy work at all levels by agencies and advertisers—costly enough mistakes to finance his kids' college educations.

"Small mistakes account for most of the problems," he said. "Giant mistakes happen whether there are contracts or not."

TOOLBOX

Make sure your agreements with subcontractors (writers, photographers, artists, musicians, etc.) completely spell out your compensation arrangement; including whether or not they get residual payments if you continue to use the work. It may prove more cost-effective to pay an additional amount up front, in exchange for a buy-out.

The Long Arm

A word on "preventative maintenance": an insurance policy can help—errors and omissions (E&O), or directors and officers (D&O—but there is no substitute for just plain doing it right. For those who think they can try to infringe on others' work "because it's too expensive to come after me," take heed. There's always someone who will fight back—on principle alone.

The late Michael J. Motto, principal of Michael J. Motto Advertising in New Providence, New Jersey, did just that. He had made a presentation to a now-defunct chain of retail appliance stores, complete with a creative campaign using a familiar character actor. The appliance stores hired another agency, but attempted to use Motto's campaign. He sued, and won.

TOOLBOX

Ad wars can be costly. Choose your battles carefully. If a competitor looks like he or she has infringed on either your product or your advertising, get competent legal and/or advertising counsel to assess both the damage done, and the potential for recovery. Moral victories don't pay well.

Stay Clean

In conclusion, just remember that if you are ever tempted to stray outside the straight and narrow path, don't. It's not worth it. You have enough to do running your business and growing your business. It's not worth violating laws and regulations. The drain on your resources will ultimately prove counterproductive. Concentrate on outthinking, outanalyzing, outmarketing, outadvertising, and finally, *outselling* your competition. It produces a much greater return on your investment.

◀◀ Time Capsule: "Eat at Perry's"

We're not going far back, on this, our last trip back for a look at another great restaurant advertising experience.

Check out the décor; it looks just like a courtroom . . . and it even *works* like one. For private parties, you can rent the judge's chambers . . . complete with a judge and bailiffs. Whenever you send anything back to the kitchen, the cook gets sentenced to dishwashing. Then, for slightly larger groups, there's the jury room. Everybody behaves incredibly well in front of the waitstaff—of course, they carry real clubs and handcuffs.

Be sure to read the disclaimer on the menu, about the management not being responsible for anything. It appears that the patrons and the staff get along just great; they leave everything to good old blind American justice. Disputes are always settled before dessert. I've seen gourmet chefs stuck scrubbing pots—lawyers, too . . . depending on the judge. Meanwhile, why do you think they list the price as fines? I'll bet they don't get a lot of word-of-mouth advertising.

Now, here's where Perry and the gang get creative. Did you see that crowd waiting in the vestibule? They all had summonses in their hands— a great traffic builder. Quickest response time of any advertising medium or message I've ever seen. See the heavily guarded group of people in the corner? Subpoenas—it works every time.

Now, as for that long line of people in the chains, they all own other restaurants in town and got convicted of unfair comparative advertising. In the basement, evildoers who tried to trade on other restaurants' goodwill are *peeling onions!*

Well, let's pay the damages—I mean the bill, and get back home.

Hey, has anyone seen my credit card? I could have sworn I had it when I came in. . . . **»**

The Highlight Zone: "In Advertising We Trust"

Submitted for your approval, a world very much like our own—at least, at first glance. We enter a large room full of people suspended above beds, each seemingly connected by wires to a machine. It seems that our subjects are in a deep, dreamlike state. Their mandate: behavior modification.

Each member of this society has a small sliver of microfilm attached to his or her index finger at birth. The microfilm has all of the allowable acts. If it's not on the microfilm, it's not permitted.

Our group of criminals has been sentenced, each for a different duration, each to a different programmed set of dreams, designed to correct future behavior.

Observe inmate 117, in the corner; one Julian Fieldstone, advertising executive. His transgression? Did he commit a serious act against the State? Like making unfair comparisons between his clients' products and those of their competitors? Did he rig a shot for a toothpaste ad, to make a smile appear whiter? No, our Mr. Fieldstone simply forgot to refer viewers to a disclaimer. He won't do it again, to be sure.

At the opposite end of the room, we find inmate 1102, one Frances Goldsmith; of late, a marketer of consumer health care products.

It seems Ms. Goldsmith has a long sentence ahead of her. Had she failed to disclose ingredients on a label? Did she produce ads and commercials deemed misleading? Or falsify demonstrations of her products? No. You see, Ms. Goldsmith simply failed to indicate that "Your results may vary." Very serious, indeed. That's her attorney, Mr. Harvey Childs, next to her. Evidently, he's missed these critical details before.

Are we too severe in our judgments, and with our punishments? Perhaps we do not have all the answers in this world. Perhaps this is a world that places the good of the many above the interests of the few. It is, after all, so much safer that way. Nobody stopped the lawmakers, so it must be the will of the people. There is no place here for the lawless.

Submitted for your consideration, the question: Have the leaders of this society gone too far? Perhaps.

THE RULES ARE CHANGING AGAIN

Most of our laws in the United States are based in principle on British common law. Fundamentally, our laws stem from early religious doctrines dating back before Moses' Ten Commandments. In fact, the Babylonian king Hammurabi's law code preceded the Bible; the Sumerian law code of Ur Nammu predated his. The oldest surviving written law code, it reveals what organized society's greatest concerns were. Have they changed? Not that much.

Sure, the content of the ancient law codes differs from today's, but the intent remains the same: to protect life, limb, and property. As always, the challenge is to achieve and maintain balance—balance between the rights and obligations of parties with differing interests.

Each of us has the right to pursue our own individual enterprise, the right to earn a profitable return on our time, material, and intellectual investment, and an obligation not to unfairly profit from the investment of another. But the lines have begun to blur.

Where it was once clear that an invention or work began here and ended there, technology has made it easy to adapt, copy, manipulate, and transform original works. The question now becomes, is the new whole greater than the sum of its parts?

If I incorporate your music, your artwork, your text into a new work, is it still your intellectual property? Do I have to compensate you for it? If I use a new medium of transfer to disseminate the work, is it still the same work? The answers are changing as you read this.

We asked our expert, Doug Wood of Reed Smith LLP, to offer some updated commentary on recent and current developments in the field of ad law. Do we see any directional shifts coming? His remarks follow.

"Without question, the most significant development in advertising law in the last five years is the collision between privacy advocates and marketers taking advantage of what technology now offers to target consumers. For decades, the protection of privacy was, at best, an afterthought in marketing regulation. In the United States, there was a long-standing view that a marketer had at least one shot at a consumer with a telephone call, a direct mail piece, or a door-to-door salesman. But then the Internet entered the marketing world and privacy suddenly became a front-burner issue. So-called 'permission marketing' was born as marketers realized that the dormant giant of privacy had awakened. Moreover, the backlash has not been limited to e-mail marketing. The privacy revolution has extended into general marketing efforts in banking, healthcare, and a myriad of other industries. Today's umbrella of privacy regulations covers a wide array of marketing efforts that has now spilled over from permission marketing to 'disclosure marketing' where efforts are afoot to force marketers to label more of their efforts as paid pitches to consumers, whether it's product placement, word of mouth, buzz, or viral. The revolution has begun and the consumer is increasingly in charge of not only what they buy but also when they'll allow marketers to talk to them."

Afterword

Now you have it all—both a roadmap and a blueprint that will help you plan, create, and execute a battle plan that will raise your business head and shoulders above the rest. It sounds so dangerous! So let's review, in brief.

Yes, market research comes first. Learn who uses your product, and what makes them tick. Find out what they buy now, how much they're willing to pay, where they shop, what's most important to them—and what it would take to make them switch to you.

Play matchmaker! Look for the media with a reader-listener-viewer profile that *matches* your ideal prospects. Remember, advertising is a *process*. Those media choices and media combinations will *change*. Use the weapons of choice that make sense for the battle *at hand*. Are you opening new markets, launching new products, protecting your turf—or just strengthening your hold on your existing trading area?

Now that you've chosen your enemies, sharpened your axes, and staked your claim, what will you *say* to your legions of followers, to keep them in your camp? Long before the fires are lit, you will compose those messages carefully—to stir their hearts and to rouse their spirits. You will speak to them in tones that resonate—and to each in their native tongues. (Yup.)

You who are wise, and who have read and understood the words in this book, will seek the counsel of learned men and women—of those who have fought such battles before. You will enter into the forest of the ad people; you will listen to their fables; and you will decide which ones can speak *your* truth to the world. You will study the campaigns they have waged, and you will *know* who can rally scores of followers to your cause. (Oy!)

When you go into battle, remember this: Many have tried; some have failed; few have won—but fewer have tried, failed, and *still* won. *You* will be among them. And *I* will be with you, because you have this book.

Be strong, be victorious, be ingenious. Face the enemy, and re-read this book until you figure out why you're still screwing up! If that doesn't work, then call me.

—Barry Cohen

Appendix A

Recommended Reading

- Caples, John, *Tested Advertising Methods,* Prentice-Hall.
- Gladwell, Malcolm, *The Tipping Point: How Little Things Can Make a Big Difference,* Back Bay Books.
- Godwin, Seth, *The Purple Cow: Transform Your Business By Being Remarkable,* Portfolio.
- Levinson, Jay, *Guerrilla Marketing,* Houghton-Mifflin.
- Levitt, Theodore, *The Marketing Imagination,* Macmillan.
- Ogilvy, David, *Ogilvy on Advertising,* Random House.
- Rapp, Stan, & Collins, Tom, *Maximarketing,* McGraw-Hill.
- Roman, Kenneth, & Maas, Jane, *How to Advertise,* St. Martin's Press.
- Trout, Jack & Ries, Al, *Marketing Warfare: How to Use Military Strategies to Develop Marketing Strategies,* McGraw-Hill.
- Trout, Jack, & Ries, Al, *Positioning: The Battle for Your Mind,* Warner Books.
- Wood, Douglas, *Please Be Ad-Vised: The Legal Reference Guide for the Advertising Executive,* Association of National Advertisers.

Appendix B

10 Ways to Screw Up an Ad Campaign Glossary

AAAA: American Association of Advertising Agencies. A trade association with membership by invitation only. This organization sets standards for its members.

Accrual: The amount of co-op advertising money earned by a dealer or distributor, from its supplier, usually based on the dollar volume of product purchased.

Advertising agency: A company that acts on behalf of your business to create, plan, place, and execute advertising for any and all of the various media.

Advertising Checking Bureau: An independent clearinghouse that checks the accuracy of and the entitlement to dealers' and distributors' claims for reimbursement of manufacturers' co-op dollars.

Affective component: The emotional element in the creative portion of your advertising.

Aftermarket: The related secondary purchases that typically follow certain major purchases. (For example, home improvement products following the purchase of a home.)

Agency review: The process of inviting, interviewing, and reviewing prospective advertising agencies to handle your company's advertising.

Aided recall: A tracking device that involves giving customers a choice of various media where they may have seen or heard your ad.

Attribution: Giving credit to specific advertising media for producing a result.

Bait and switch: A deceptive and often illegal practice that involves enticing people with an advertised item, then attempting to sell them a different one (usually at a higher price).

Banner: A prominent ad on an Internet that usually runs across the top of the pages.

Barriers to entry: Conditions that impede your ability to penetrate a market.

Barter: The practice of trading your goods and services for other goods and services, rather than purchasing them with cash.

Big idea: A theme on which you can hang a continuing ad campaign on.

Brand awareness: The level of public awareness of the existence and attributes of a product or a product line.

Brand preference: The level of public acceptance and endorsement of a specific branded item or product line.

Buyer's remorse: When consumers feel uneasy after making a major purchase. Marketers must have a strategy in place to address it.

Call to action: The element in the ad that asks consumers to do something—buy, call, visit, or click.

Cause-related marketing: When an advertiser allies his or her business with a socially responsible effort through sponsorships, etc.

Centers of influence: Community leaders with influence over a particular circle of people.

Circulation: The total number of people receiving a publication, including newsstand sales plus subscriptions.

Click-through: The act of opening a banner ad, pop-up, or otherelement on an Internet page; also refers to the response rate to an Internet ad.

Cloning: A direct marketing technique that involves advertising to prospects similar to a given customer profile (with like demographics or special interests).

Coat-tail: The act of capitalizing on someone else's successful advertising.

Co-op advertising: When a supplier gives advertising dollars to its distributors and dealers, sharing the cost of advertising its products with them.

Copyright: Federal and international law that protects the specific expression of ideas—musical compositions and recordings, films, photographs, artwork, written works, advertisements, etc.

Cost per lead (cost per response): A way to measure ad costs based on the cost to reach each respondent.

Cost-reach ratio: A way to measure ad costs based on the cost to reach each (target) person.

Creative: The process of devising the look, sound, and actual text of your ads. Also refers to the actual completed ad campaign—the execution of your message.

Crisis intervention: A form of public relations designed to mitigate the impact of negative publicity on your business.

Crosscheck: A way to further prompt customers to see what advertising influenced them. To check the accuracy of their answers to both aided and unaided recall, it involves asking them what media they usually read, watch, or listen to.

Cross-promote: When you and other businesses agree to promote one another to each other's customers.

Customer profile: A description of the characteristics of your customers—their geographic and demographic makeup.

Data capture: The ability to secure information about customers or prospects responding to an ad.

Delivery system: The method used to get your product from the producer to the consumer.

Demographics: The socioeconomic characteristics of a population—age, race, sex, income, and ethnic make-up.

De-selectors: Elements that make people not want to respond favorably to a communication. These may include a spokesperson's face, voice, body type, or accent.

Direct response: Advertising in various media designed to generate telephone, mail, or Internet orders and inquiries—not to generate store traffic or to build brand awareness.

Disclaimer: A statement appearing in an ad that disavows responsibility or liability for something.

Disclosure: A statement in an ad that alerts the consumer to information affecting a purchasing decision.

Dot-com: A company using e-commerce (Internet) as its primary business model.

Errors and omissions insurance: Offers some degree of liability protection to an advertiser or advertising agency against unintentional mistakes.

Event marketing: When an advertiser sponsors a special event to gain credibility and patronage.

Fragmentation: The division of a population by different audience characteristics. It results in the need for a mixed-media campaign to reach each of the divergent subgroups.

Freelancer: An independent advertising practitioner, usually with a particular area of specialization.

Frequency: The number of times an ad is seen or heard by a reader, viewer, or listener.

Generation X: The current generation of younger adult consumers, ages 25–40.

Generation Y: The current generation of teens and young adults, up to age 25.

Heavy users: People who purchase more of your product, or purchase it more often.

Hyperbole: Poetic exaggeration used for effect in advertising copy.

Hyperlink: Allows a consumer to connect from one Internet location directly to another.

Identity: The unique "signature" or "fingerprint" that belongs to your enterprise alone; how you portray your business to the world.

Influencer: A person with input into a purchasing decision, although he or she may not make the final purchasing decision or the actual transaction.

Insertion: Each appearance of a print ad in a given publication.

Institutional advertising: Advertising designed to increase the company or the brand's awareness level; nonpromotional advertising.

Jargon: Industry-specific or technical language not understood by the general population.

Jingle: A musical commercial for radio or television; an extremely powerful device to create brand identity and memorability.

Knockoff: A product that imitates a popular branded item; often sold for less.

Last reference: The last place a customer recalls seeing or hearing your advertising—not necessarily the only place motivating him or her to respond.

List broker: A company or individual who resells (or rents) mailing lists from a variety of sources.

Loss leader: An item advertised at an extremely low price, usually below wholesale, in an effort to attract consumers to purchase other items.

Market research: The fact-finding process used by marketers to discover information about consumer habits and preferences required to properly execute an advertising campaign.

Marriage mailing: When advertisers send their mailings out together, co-operatively, and share the cost.

Media: The various means of communication available to advertise your business—radio, TV, magazines, newspapers, billboards, direct mail, Internet, etc. It also refers to the actual space or time you buy.

Minimalism: Forms of expression that use the sparsest of elements, where "less is more"; no unnecessary details.

Mixed media: An ad campaign using a combination of two or more different advertising media at the same time. It reaches more people, and may also reach the same people more times, depending on how much audience duplication the various media have.

Mnemonic device: A sound or other device by which people will remember and identify your ads, and ultimately, associate your business with.

Model's (talent) release: An instrument securing permission to use an individual's likeness or voice in your advertising. It indemnifies the studio, photographer, videographer, ad agency, and advertiser against claims for additional compensation for hired models, actors, and other talent.

Monumental graphics: A style of artwork appearing larger than life; it "bursts off the page"—recommended for outdoor ads viewed at a distance.

Newsgroup: Internet site involving focused online discussion groups on specific topics.

Offline promotion: Using traditional (non-Internet) media to drive traffic to a Web site.

Online promotion: Advertising on the Internet itself, using banners, hyperlinks, newsgroups, pop-ups, e-mail, etc.

Opportunistic advertising: A form of advertising that takes advantage of a genuine advertising value, like quality unsold time or space at reduced rates. It may also involve a contingency arrangement (such as running ads only at times when conditions suit you).

Out-of-home: Advertising that includes billboards, mass transit, airport, and other forms of indoor and outdoor advertising that reach people away from the home.

Page dominant: A print ad that is larger than a half page, yet less than a full page. It dwarfs any ads run around it, but may also be surrounded with editorial matter. These ads command attention without the advertiser paying for a full page.

Pass-along readership: Additional, secondary readers per copy of a publication, over and above subscribers and newsstand purchasers. (Added together, all of the above give you the true circulation.)

Patent: Federal law granting protection to a unique invention or process.

Per-inquiry (P.I.) advertising: A way for the media to liquidate unsold space or time. The advertiser only pays for each actual response to the ads.

Perceived value: What the consumer believes a product or service is worth.

Personification: Giving human qualities to an inanimate object in your ad.

Pop-up: A similar device to an Internet banner ad; however, usually smaller.

Product position: The position your product occupies in the consumer's mind, relative to your competitors. The term also refers to how you position your product's attributes against that of its competitors.

Production company: A company often acting as a subcontractor to an advertising agency; it performs the actual technical work required to produce your ads and commercials.

Production value: The level of quality in the execution of your ads, ranging from high to low.

Promotion: A form of advertising designed to generate response through an exciting, time-sensitive offer—usually either off-price merchandise or a contest of some type.

Proximity effect: Capitalizing on a last-minute media exposure to influence a purchase.

Public relations: Communication designed to create a favorable climate for sales by promulgating positive information.

Pulsing: An advertising schedule consisting of a light, steady maintenance program, plus added advertising during key or peak sales periods.

Reach: The number of people who actually see or hear an ad during the course of a schedule. (It amounts to a percentage of the total readership, viewership, or listenership.)

Readership: The total number of people who actually read a given publication. It may exceed circulation, allowing for pass-along readership.

Regressive discount: A technique to induce customers to respond more quickly; it involves a decreasing discount the longer they wait to use it.

Repositioning: Refocusing marketing strategy by refocusing attention on how the product satisfies different consumer needs. For example, when Arm & Hammer Baking Soda achieved near saturation levels of market penetration, they needed to get people to buy additional units of product. The answer: one box for your refrigerator smells; another to clean carpet stains or brush your teeth.

Robinson-Patman Act: A law designed to ensure fair and equitable distribution of manufacturers' co-op advertising dollars.

Satire: Also known as parody; involves ridiculing a real-life situation or another existing creative work. It is seldom used to sell product.

Solo mailing: The term for an advertiser sending out a mailing as a stand-alone piece.

Specifier: The person who actually makes a purchasing decision-although he or she may not make the actual purchase transaction.

Strategic alliance: Agreement to work together with other businesses to achieve a common goal; may include sharing or exchanging services.

Subscribership: The number of people paying to receive delivery of an advertising medium. It does not guarantee readership, viewership, or actual noting or recall of an ad.

Trade secret: A secret process or product attribute unique to that product, and known by only a small number of people.

Trademark: Words, logos, symbols, and slogans that identify the origin of a product.

Trading area: A business's usual and customary geographic service area.

Trigger event: A life-changing situation that results in motivating a purchase—birth, death, moving, adoption, retirement, etc.

Unaided recall: A market research technique that involves asking customers to volunteer information—such as where they saw or heard your advertising—without prompting them with suggestions or choices.

Unique selling proposition: An attributes that differentiates your product, service, or establishment from the competition.

Value-added: A term for something additional that your business adds to a product or service to make it more enticing to consumers.

Vendor support: Discretionary supplier money to help fund dealer promotions.

Work on spec: The term for an ad agency, freelancer, production company, or media outlet preparing an ad or a campaign on speculation, before the advertiser commits to working with them.

Index

A

Ad agencies, 11–20, 30–39. *See also* Freelancers
Adams, Dennis, 26
Adlaw by Request, 225–26
Advertising campaign, 5, 31–32, 41–44, 68–75, 198–224
Advertising costs, 11, 15, 147–50, 183–97
Advertising IQ, 102–8
Advertising law, 109–10, 203, 225–48
Advertising medium, 12, 20, 31, 37–39, 68, 78–81, 112, 153–82
Advertising needs, 102–17
Advertising results, 42–43, 68–75, 120–31
Advertising strategies, 23–29
Advertising yardstick, 121, 123
Aladdin, 232
Allied Old English, 200
American Express, 168
Anchor Concrete, 51
Apparel advertising, 194–95
AT&T, 94

B

"Bait and switch" tactics, 23
Barry Herman Entertainment, 196
Barter ads, 38
BBD&O, 103
Benefits versus features, 70–72, 103, 126
Bienvenue, Richard, 40, 180
Billboards, 146–47, 165–66, 186
Bose, 106
Bounty, 84
Brand awareness, 42–43
Brand identity, 94, 105–6
Brunswick Corporation, 97
Budget-stretchers, 183–97
Business cards, 195

C

Caples, John, 103
Capps Companies, 16
Capps, Martha, 16–17
Car advertising, 193
Cargo Logistics, 78–79
Carlin, George, 228
Caroline, Peter, 14, 81, 86
Carroll, Jerry, 84
Catalogs, 48–49, 169, 173–74
Central Holidays, 107
Chevrolet, 3, 213
Clairol, 3

About the Author

Barry Cohen began his advertising career over twenty-seven years ago, at a 1,000-watt radio station. He has worked on both the media side and the ad agency side of the business. For about ten of those years, he has operated his own ad agency. He has also served as a general manager of a commercial radio station.

Mr. Cohen holds a Bachelor of Arts in English cum laude from Kean University (1975) and has addressed numerous business groups, including chambers of commerce, trade associations, and conferences on the subject of effective advertising. He holds seven creative awards, including those given by the Dynamic Graphics Foundation, the New Jersey Ad Club, Communications Advertising & Marketing Association, and the prestigious national Silver Microphone Awards.

Listed in *Who's Who Among Students in American Universities & Colleges*, as well as *Outstanding Young Americans* and *Lexington's Who's Who in Business*, he has been employed at the flagship stations of both Park Communications and the Buckley Broadcasting Corporation. Currently, he serves as principal of AdLab Media Communications, LLC, an ad agency/audio-video production company.

Focused on results, Mr. Cohen has numerous promotional successes to his credit, including a campaign for an auto dealer that sold 187 cars in five days; a one-week restaurant promotion that attracted 856 documented responses; a concert sellout in two weeks; the generation of 1,000 leads for a major cruise line; a two-month campaign that achieved a 50 percent sales increase for a home improvement products manufacturer; the garnering of 1,458 leads for a nutritional supplement in one month; and he also takes credit for creating a horrendous rush-hour traffic jam at a highway furniture store.

Visual communications have included a slide show that resulted in a $600 million capital improvement grant, a prospectus that generated financing for a $1.4 million acquisition, and the cover photo for a bank annual report.

His publicity successes include placements for a national brokerage firm in the top spot of *The New Jersey Law Journal*, a statewide professional journal; a prominent article in *The Star-Ledger*, New Jersey's largest newspaper; and appearances on radio and television talk shows, including *A Current Affair*.

Contact the author at barry@adlabcreative.com.